"As a registered dietitian specialized in eating disorders who has been in this field for over three decades, I can wholeheartedly say that FINALLY, a book that courageously, compassionately, and collaboratively brings a controversial issue – veganism and eating disorders – to the forefront is here! Jenn Friedman walks the reader through where we are now as a profession, what our challenges continue to be, and where we need to go in spite of and because of any differences we, as clinicians, may have within our own opinions and beliefs. Friedman graciously asks all of us to bring our beliefs and prejudices around veganism and eating disorders towards the light so the shadows of misunderstanding can be seen, heard, discussed, and healed. I recommend this enlightening book, and its guidelines on how to become vegan-informed, to any and all practicing clinicians who work with clients who have eating disorders in general and who practice veganism specifically."

Tammy Beasley, MS, RDN, CEDS-S, LD

"Jenn Friedman has done a great job in this book by challenging therapists to examine their own socially-supported bias and unconscious prejudice against veganism, that inevitably interferes with the therapeutic alliance. She draws on a wide range of literature to highlight the separation between an individual's chaotic relationship with eating and the philosophical and ethical stance of not eating animals. This book dispels the myth that veganism is an eating disorder variant whilst highlighting the important distinction between the mental and existential anguish of vystopia and the philosophical basis upon which a vegan lives their life."

Clare Mann, *psychologist and author of* Vystopia: The Anguish of Being Vegan in a Non-Vegan World

VEGANISM AND EATING DISORDER RECOVERY

This book addresses the eating disorder field's misconceptions about veganism with the goal of realigning the discourse about veganism and non-veganism in eating disorder recovery.

Veganism and eating disorders are often associated with one another in the eating disorder field, leading to the widely adopted belief that following the dietary component of veganism may inhibit recovery from an eating disorder. Friedman posits that this belief is founded on an oversimplified view and counters it by exploring the ethical dimensions of veganism. In this book, Friedman looks at ideas perpetuated around veganism and recovery, including the potential harm to vegans prohibited from following veganism in treatment centers. *Veganism and Eating Disorder Recovery* culminates in a prospective proposal for a "vegan-informed" eating disorder recovery model, which may be adapted for clients' individual needs.

Friedman lays a foundation for an improved discourse on veganism and eating disorders by drawing from a wide range of resources, including academic research, blog posts, eating disorder literature, and anecdotes. This accessible text will appeal to professionals and eating disorder clients alike, enabling them to collaborate under optimal conditions.

Jenn Friedman, MA, MHC-LP, obtained her counseling master's degree at Goldsmiths, University of London and New York State licensure prerequisites at the University of Buffalo. She provides therapy in New York City.

VEGANISM AND EATING DISORDER RECOVERY

Jenn Friedman
Edited by Louise Tucker

Routledge
Taylor & Francis Group

NEW YORK AND LONDON

Cover image: Getty Image

First published 2023
by Routledge
605 Third Avenue, New York, NY 10158

and by Routledge
4 Park Square, Milton Park, Abingdon, Oxon, OX14 4RN

Routledge is an imprint of the Taylor & Francis Group, an informa business

Library of Congress Cataloging-in-Publication Data
Names: Friedman, Jenn, author.
Title: Veganism and eating disorder recovery / by Jenn Friedman.
Description: First edition. | New York, NY : Routledge, 2023. |
    Includes bibliographical references and index.
Identifiers: LCCN 2022027793 (print) | LCCN 2022027794 (ebook) |
    ISBN 9781032316246 (hbk) | ISBN 9781032316239 (pbk) |
    ISBN 9781003310617 (ebk)
Subjects: LCSH: Eating disorders—Diet therapy. | Veganism.
Classification: LCC RC552.E18 F74 2023 (print) | LCC RC552.E18 (ebook) |
    DDC 616.85/260654—dc23/eng/20220716
LC record available at https://lccn.loc.gov/2022027793
LC ebook record available at https://lccn.loc.gov/2022027794

ISBN: 978-1-032-31624-6 (hbk)
ISBN: 978-1-032-31623-9 (pbk)
ISBN: 978-1-003-31061-7 (ebk)

DOI: 10.4324/9781003310617

Typeset in Joanna MT
by Apex CoVantage, LLC

CONTENTS

About the Author   ix
Preface   x
Acknowledgments   xiii

Introduction   1

Section I   Establishing Where We Are   **13**

1   My Story: Eating Disorder Treatment and Veganism   15

2   An Uncomfortable Task Ahead   21

3   Public Perception at a Glance   27

4   Recovery Perspectives   34

5   The Importance of Understanding Motivation for Veganism   47

Section II   Vegan Experiences   **59**

6   Conflating Concepts: Perfectionism, Morality, Freedom   61

7 Veganism's Traumatic Roots   70

8 Implications of Non-Vegan Eating Disorder Treatment   77

9 Losing Veganism   86

10 Animal Therapy in Non-Vegan Eating Disorder Treatment   96

11 Identity   103

Section III   A Way Forward   **111**

12 Professionally Considering a Patient's Veganism   113

13 Working with Ambivalence and Values   127

14 The Therapeutic Alliance   139

15 Co-constructing a Broader Way Forward   145

16 Professional Communication Throughout Different Levels of Care   152

17 Professional Self-Reflective Practice   158

18 Proposing a Vegan-Informed Approach   166

Conclusion   177

Index   182

ABOUT THE AUTHOR

Jenn Friedman, MA, MHC-LP, is a counselor, author, and musician. She obtained her advanced graduate mental health counseling certificate from the University at Buffalo and her master's degree in Counseling from Goldsmiths University of London, where she trained in psycho-dynamic therapy. She also holds a certification in creative arts and health from the New School for Social Research. Friedman provides therapy in New York City. Her approach to counseling is informed by psycho-dynamic and cognitive principles.

Friedman has loved creating written and musical work since she was a child. After studying music composition at SUNY Purchase and going through her personal mental health recovery journey, she authored *Eating Disorders on the Wire: Music and Metaphor as Pathways to Recovery* (H.T.F.K. Press) and recorded its coinciding album, *On the Wire* (Personal Bias Records). She has performed her work at various musical venues and mental health events.

Friedman has been practicing veganism for many years and is deeply supportive of the vegan movement. Originally from Brooklyn, she currently lives with her partner in their Manhattan apartment.

For information about *Veganism and Eating Disorder Recovery*, please visit https://eatingdisordersandveganism.com/

For information about Jenn's music and previous publication, please visit https://jennfriedman.com/

PREFACE

I began writing this book after coming across a retweet of a *Washington Post* article about eating disorder treatment and veganism called "Perspective: Eating Disorders and Veganism: Is there a link?" (Dennett, 2020). Despite my having rarely read an article whose premise opined anything other than "affirmative," I noticed that the original tweet said, "Although the diet is restrictive, it can be followed in a healthful way." This piqued my interest, so I read on to see that the retweet was from Alsana, an eating disorder treatment facility providing inpatient and outpatient services. The retweet said, "Alsana is one of few eatingdisorder treatment centers that accept ethical vegan patients and allow them to remain vegan" (Alsana, 2020).

Although I had heard through secondary sources that certain treatment centers allowed vegan meals, I had never—in my history of sickness, advocacy, academia, or professional experience—come across a statement by an eating disorder treatment center in support of a patient's preference to remain vegan in treatment. Therefore, seeing a treatment center proactively appeal to vegans was the breath of fresh air I had long been awaiting. Having been duly inspired, I began writing what I thought would be a Facebook status. However, the would-be post quickly outgrew its Facebook destination and became more like an essay. Soon thereafter, I found myself knee deep in research and so it expanded once more, outgrowing its "essay" status by a hefty margin. It grew and grew, and I engaged with it more and more intensely each passing day and now, here we are: it's a bloody book (no, I'm not British—just enjoying the residual effects of having lived in London for two years).

In my research, I came across the website of Valerie Martin, LCSW, RYT, who calls herself "the Vegan Therapist." This description really struck me because up till then, I had never known a therapist to specifically identify as vegan. In fact, this had been on my mind for a while, being a therapist myself. The questions of what to disclose versus what not to disclose to prospective clients had been rumbling around in my brain since I started my counseling master's in London in 2017. So, sufficiently intrigued, I visited Martin's blog and noticed the following section of her post:

> At a networking dinner during my first year as a vegan, I nervously disclosed my recent change to an ED dietitian sitting next to me. The restaurant had been graciously accommodating and prepared special options for me as an alternative to their signature seafood. The dietitian said to me, "I wouldn't tell people that if I were you." I'll never forget that moment, and while I know that her feelings are not representative of the entire field, it's not the only time I've heard comments like this. I am determined to raise awareness within the field, and encourage clinicians to carefully explore this with each individual in order to distinguish between disordered behaviors and choices made for ethical reasons, and direct treatment accordingly.
> (Martin, 2019)

I was taken by Martin's post for multiple reasons. Firstly, I can understand why this dietitian's comment had an impact. Secondly, while I agree that the comment was not representative of the field, I have heard such comments myself. Lastly, like Martin, I believe that eating disorders and vegan ethics ought to be responsibly explored on an individual basis to provide the best treatment for any one person. I am therefore at once relieved to see someone else talking about this and disheartened at the need for it to be talked about. And with that, here I am, talking about it.

References

Alsana. [@alsanallc]. (2020, July 19). Alsana is one of few #eatingdisorder treatment centers that accept ethical vegan patients and allow them to remain #vegan. [Tweet]. *Twitter.* https://twitter.com/alsanallc/status/1284958689011662858

Dennett, Carrie. (2020, July 16). Veganism and eating disorders: Is there a link? *The Washington Post.* www.washingtonpost.com/lifestyle/wellness/veganism-and-eating-disorders-is-there-a-link/2020/07/15/0f5fbd44-c6cd-11ea-8ffe-372be8d82298_story.html

Martin, V. (2019, July 24). Busting myths about veganism: Part 1. *Val the Vegan Therapist.* www.valthevegantherapist.com/blog/busting-vegan-myths-1

ACKNOWLEDGMENTS

I deeply value the support that has been extended to me throughout the process of writing and publishing this book.

Thank you, Sally Fricker, for your hugely impactful feedback at the very start. Thank you, Heidi Dalzell, Kel O'Neill, and Kate Goldston for your incredible generosity and affirmation. Thank you, Christine Jackson, for offering such thoughtful and dedicated feedback on the manuscript. Thank you, Tammy Beasley, for your encouragement, zest, and feedback through and through.

Thank you, Melainie Rogers, Valerie Martin, Leslie Davenport, Clare Mann, Jenny Weinar, and Dallas Rising for our affirming, heart-opening conversations at various stages of this work. Your alignment with this work has reignited the flame over and over.

Thank you, Anneliese Kappey, for your unconditional presence. Thank you for caring about this book at every stage and for the trusted feedback you so graciously provided.

Thank you to my friends near and far for your expressions of support throughout this journey, especially Randi Feuer, Vanessa Unkeless-Perez, Katie Louccheim, and Meredith Villano.

Thank you, Adrienne, for your faith and support since the beginning.

I am thankful to the eating disorder recovery community for its tireless work toward helping people recover. Thank you to those with whom I've walked/performed/lobbied. Thank you to those who have helped me through my own recovery journey.

I would like to extend my gratitude toward the vegan community for its loyalty and persistence in advocating for animal rights. Thank you especially to the Ethical Vegan Mental Health Providers group, including Beth Levine, Lisa Levinson, and Jean Shirkoff for your enthusiastic support of this book. I would also like to thank the Vegans of New York Facebook group for its dedicated communal activism.

I am grateful to the Goldsmiths faculty, especially Lynne Brown and Maya Mukamel, for supporting my development as a training therapist. I am thankful to the University at Buffalo faculty for teaching me counseling skills to integrate into my practice. I hold my academic colleagues and confidantes close to my heart. Special thanks to Alice, Sarah, and Liz for your support and friendship throughout our training.

Thank you to my past and present clinical supervisors, Damian Castello, Jenny Rella, and Michal Tzyion, for helping me cultivate my personal and professional growth.

Thank you to my editor, Louise Tucker, for your insight and mentorship. Thanks for believing in this book as much as I do! With your help, it has transformed into what I've always intended it to be.

Thank you to Amanda Savage, Katya Porter, and the team at Routledge/ CRC Press for this incredible opportunity. I am over the moon!

To my partner, Ben: thank you for your unconditional support, encouragement, and love throughout this process. I've trusted it completely.

Thank you to my family and Ben's family. Thank you to my mom, Irene, and my dad, Alan, for your love, support, and encouragement. Special thanks to my cousin, Sam.

Finally, thank you to music for picking me up again and again.

INTRODUCTION

Veganism and eating disorders are often presumed to be associated with one another in the therapeutic/professional/academic eating disorder field, leading to the widely adopted belief that following the dietary component of veganism may inhibit recovery from an eating disorder. I consider it important to become curious about how this association has occurred and why many people in the eating disorder field adopt the idea that veganism presents an inherent barrier to recovery.

The prevailing narrative that veganism is ill advised in eating disorder recovery potentially contributes to compromising a vegan's treatment in a facility via unnecessary psychological pain; preventing someone from getting treatment at all; and/or preventing someone from realizing that adhering to the dietary component of veganism is not in their best interest.

DOI: 10.4324/9781003310617-1

In this book, I address the eating disorder field's misconceptions about veganism with the goal of expanding the discourse on veganism in eating disorder recovery. In doing so, I apply my mental health counseling experience—alongside my personal experiences with veganism and eating disorder recovery—toward exploring current perspectives of veganism in the eating disorder field and subsequent recovery approaches; flaws in some of the existing research on eating disorders and veganism; vegan perspectives as they pertain to various aspects of eating disorders; the potential risk to vegans when they are prohibited from eating vegan in treatment centers; potential for unconscious vegan bias among those involved in a vegan client's care; and considerations in adopting a more holistic and supportive approach.

Many in the eating disorder field consider veganism to be a rationale for eating disordered restriction. By extension, because of the obvious fact that an eating disorder sufferer's health ought to come first, many believe that veganism must come second. However, this logic neglects to account for a few in-between steps.

It is true that health and recovery are vital. However, if the accepted norm in the eating disorder field is that veganism does not equate to health, then the implication will be that veganism is secondary to recovery—a notion that renders a person's recovery fundamentally compromised. Even if professionals believe that a patient is vegan for ethical reasons, any mistrust of veganism as it pertains to recovery can still factor into (and potentially mar) the patient's treatment.

If veganism is automatically deemed a less healthy option across the board, then—no matter the patient's values—non-vegan eating would appear to be the best way forward. There are multiple explanations for this, many of which come from a compassionate place.

With that, I am aware that clinicians, first and foremost, have a duty to protect their clients. Because of this, they base their decisions on the ethical principles of beneficence (defined by the American Counseling Association (ACA) as "working for the good of the individual and society by promoting mental health and well-being") and nonmaleficence (defined by the ACA as "avoiding actions that cause harm") (ACA, 2014, p. 3). Likewise, the American Psychological Association (APA) lists the ethical principle of "beneficence and nonmaleficence," in which "psychologists strive to benefit those with whom they work and take care to do no harm" (APA, 2017, p. 3). Since many clinicians believe that changing their stance on veganism would be harmful to patients, they hold true to their existing beliefs.

I assume that professionals are coming from a place of the ethical principles of both nonmaleficence and beneficence when formulating, sharing, and implementing their views. Furthermore, I do not judge any view held by any professional with regard to a particular client. In fact, the point of this book is to specifically *not* dismiss individual experience or perception. The point, rather, is to address the generalization of these views both within and beyond the eating disorder field.

I, too, want to eliminate the prospect of harm, but via an individualized treatment approach toward an eating disordered person's veganism. In my view, individualizing treatment means regarding the client as both *unique* and *whole*. Each of these descriptors acknowledges that an eating disordered client still has *agency*—a healthy part of themselves that makes them who they are and that connotes their ability to make healthy decisions on their own behalf. My hope is that a clinical determination about a patient's veganism is founded upon earnest attempts at identifying the eating disordered person's agency. Such identification necessitates understanding the individual client. Viewing veganism within this framework will enable both avoidance of possible harm and provision of beneficial treatment. It will also incorporate the ethical principle of autonomy to the greatest extent possible, which the ACA defines as "fostering the right to control the direction of one's life" (ACA, 2014, p. 3). There may or may not be legitimate concern that following a vegan diet could pose harm to a particular client's recovery. However, I hold that veganism in recovery is an issue of nuance rather than consensus. As such, I position myself on neither a vegan nor a non-vegan side but rather on the side of the vegan eating disordered individual's best interest—whatever form it may take.

The therapy field might consider such an individualized treatment approach as a means toward "meeting the client where they are" in which therapists convey non-judgmental acknowledgment of clients as they are. A therapist who "meets the client where they are" conveys their fundamental acceptance of the client and works with the client from that mutually acknowledged space. "Meeting the client where they are" in the beginning of treatment may set the stage for a client to feel equally "met" throughout the therapeutic process.

This therapeutic principle applies to eating disordered patients as much as it does to any other patient. However, founder and CEO of BALANCE Eating Disorder Treatment Center™ Melainie Rogers, MS, RDN, CDN, CED-S, says that the nutritional field ought to "meet the client where they are" in the same way the therapy field does (M. Rogers, personal communication, March 12, 2022). Similarly, Senior Nutrition Leadership at Accanto Health, the parent company of The Emily Program and Veritas Collaborative, says,

> Those who come to our care having made a shift away from their family table or cultural origin toward vegetarianism or vegan diets, are met where they are and the choice of a vegetarian/vegan lifestyle is explored as a therapeutic area of interest within the eating disorder care.
>
> (Accanto Health, n.d.)

Rogers's and Accanto's sentiments matter because nutritional support is a vital part of an eating disordered patient's overall treatment.

Just as therapists aim to meet clients where they are, so does this book aim to meet the eating disorder profession where it is. I assume that all professionals will treat each client on an individual basis with nuance and sensitivity. To that end, I hold that recognizing and working with nuance is vital in determining patients' optimal treatment. Working with nuance also means that, for any number of reasons, it may not be in a patient's best interest to eat vegan in recovery. This book, as such, will help professionals as well as general readers to understand the challenges that a vegan person who is not eating vegan in recovery might face.

With that in mind, this book aims to build in a pause where an otherwise instinctive conclusion about veganism's impact on recovery may be drawn. It creates space for speculation in place of an assumption about veganism meaning lower health. It also creates space for considering what is best for each individual client. This book is an introduction to forming a better understanding of veganism and eating disorders. It is a prompt to make decisions on a case-by-case basis according to what is best for each individual patient. It is neither prescriptive nor instructional; rather, it is an attempt to legitimize veganism for eating disordered individuals who align with it; give veganism equal weight in a discussion about effective treatment; and foster an understanding about veganism's co-existence with the eating disorder field. The concepts discussed throughout this book will culminate in a prospective proposal for a "vegan-informed" model, a conceptual framework which can be adapted according to a particular patient's needs.

I have divided this book into three sections: I. "Establishing Where we Are," in which I identify and discuss current perceptions of eating disorders in conjunction with veganism; II. "Vegan Experiences," in which I discuss how experiences that are specific to vegans may impact vegans who have eating disorders; and III. "A Way Forward," in which I discuss the current climate of eating disorder treatment as a whole, issues that impact treatment providers, and the potential for a proactive future.

By the end of this book, it will be evident why the narrative around eating disorders and veganism would benefit from a major shift. Furthermore, it will be evident how this shift can positively impact a vegan's access to treatment, the quality of their treatment, and a professional's capacity to provide optimal treatment. It will also be made evident how such a shift will broaden the understanding of vegan eating disordered individuals' loved ones, foster mental health advocacy organizations' intra- and inter-personal sharing of acquired knowledge, and enrich lecturers' delivery of topical information to students. I believe that the eating disorder field will benefit from this information. By extension, I believe that anyone who is curious about eating disorders on any level will benefit from this book because it addresses a mainstream perception of eating disorders.

Definitions and Distinctions

Throughout this book, distinctions between eating disorders and veganism will be drawn. Readers should bear in mind:

- An eating disorder is a mental health condition; therefore, eating disordered behaviors are pathological.
- Veganism is an ethical philosophy; therefore, vegan behaviors are non-pathological. According to Dr. Shiri Raz, (The International

Association for Relational Psychoanalysis and Psychotherapy, Sydney, 2017), "Vegetarianism and veganism are not pathological or any form of mental disorders, they are not a cause for mental disorders nor characteristic of people with depression or mood disorders."

- An eating disorder is not primarily about food but rather psychological issues.
- Veganism is also not primarily about food because it is a philosophy that affects every part of life, including but not limited to food, e.g., clothes, bags, shampoo, etc.

In order to discuss how definitions have been either conflated or misinterpreted, it is important to highlight the following terms: eating disorders, veganism, vegetarianism, and plant-based diet.

Eating Disorders: According to the fifth edition of the *Diagnostic and Statistical Manual of Mental Disorders* (DSM-5), eating disorder diagnoses include: anorexia nervosa, bulimia nervosa, binge eating disorder, other specified feeding or eating disorder (OSFED), unspecified feeding or eating disorder (UFED), avoidant/restrictive food intake disorder (ARFID), pica, and rumination disorder (American Psychiatric Association, 2013). Of equal importance is orthorexia "in which the person becomes pathologically obsessed with eating healthy food" (Fuller et al., 2021, p. 2). Orthorexia, while not listed in the DSM-5, is nonetheless a term recognized by clinicians (National Eating Disorders Association). Among these diagnoses, the most commonly discussed are anorexia, bulimia, binge eating disorder, OSFED, and orthorexia; however, ARFID has been entering the common discourse as well.

Veganism "is a way of living which seeks to exclude, as far as is possible and practicable, all forms of exploitation of, and cruelty to, animals for food, clothing or any other purpose" (The Vegan Society). Echoing this sentiment, Brown et al. (2019, p. 2) define veganism as "a way of living based on the principle of avoiding animal use as much as possible, encompassing both dietary and non-dietary choices." Just as a vegan will not eat the flesh of a chicken, nor will they eat the chicken's eggs. Just as a vegan will not eat the flesh of a cow, nor will they drink the milk that came from the cow. Vegans will also not buy products made from or tested on animals or support institutions that profit from animal exploitation for entertainment.

Vegetarianism is the practice of not eating animal flesh. According to the Vegetarian Society (vegsoc.org), "vegetarians don't eat fish, meat, or chicken." A vegetarian will, however, eat animal by-products, such as the eggs from a chicken or the milk from a cow.

"Plant-based diet" refers to eating a diet comprised of mainly plant-based food. Whereas veganism refers to ethics, "plant-based" refers to diet alone (Root the Future, 2020; Panoff, 2020). A Root of the Future article says, "A plant-based diet consists mostly or entirely of plant-based food. A plant-based diet is more flexible than a vegan diet and may include small amounts of animal products when plant-based foods are not available." I speculate that this is because "plant-based" is frequently associated with health motivations, in which case "consumption of very small amounts of animal foods can be inconsequential when speaking of the health benefits of a diet" (Wendel, 2019). Wendel adds, "The term ['plant-based'] is divorced from any ethical connotation . . . and it doesn't mean 'never eating meat' or 'never eating animal products.'" This isn't to say that vegans cannot be motivated by health, but there is still an ethical component involved in their decision.

I ask readers to keep the distinctions between eating disorders, vegetarianism, veganism, and plant-based diets in mind while this book. The terms can further the understanding of what eating disorders are and are not as well as what veganism is and is not.

In this book, I will be referring to recovery and treatment in a variety of contexts. "Recovery" in this case is an umbrella term for anyone with an eating disorder who is at any point along the process of addressing their eating disorder. A person may be just starting to contemplate their own recovery, be farther into their recovery, or be experiencing a relapse; they may choose treatment or experience their treatment as being involuntary. They may have conflicting feelings about recovery at any point in the process. Recovery is not linear, and there are no markers by which the collective eating disordered population can be deemed to have recovered. Recovery, unlike the process of diagnosing the eating disorder, does not fit into certain categories or codes. How a person lives in recovery is as individual as the person themselves. Additionally, some people choose to call themselves "recovered" while others choose to say they are continually "in recovery." Regardless of the term a person chooses, the aim of recovery is to obtain a state of freedom from one's eating disorder, such that their quality of life is no longer impacted by eating disordered thoughts and feelings.

Recovery may accompany treatment. There are many different types of eating disorder treatment, referred to by professionals as "levels of care" (LoC). This book mostly focuses on treatment some-where within these various levels of care, including but not limited to intensive outpatient or outpatient, "partial hospitalization," resi-dential treatment, and inpatient treatment (National Eating Disorders Association, n.d.).

Any of these levels of care may transition toward, overlap with, or collaborate with any of the others. The treatment professionals involved in the client's care may consist of a therapist, a dietitian, a psychiatrist, a social worker (potentially separate from the primary therapist), an occupational therapist, a medical doctor and other medical staff, and different types of group facilitators. Depending on the level of care, these professionals may be involved in the patient's treatment to varying degrees. Oftentimes, the group of individuals involved in a patient's treatment is referred to as the patient's "treatment team." Sometimes, this team will be automatically consolidated, such as in an inpatient or intensive outpatient setting that has all staff on site for purposes of client collaboration; and sometimes this team will be comprised of individual professionals working in a variety of practices. In the latter case, it is important that each member of the team forge connections with the other members of the team so that everyone involved in the patient's care is aware of the patient's status and needs.

When discussing a person's recovery throughout this book, I assume that readers will adapt my statements to the applicable level of care and its corresponding professionals. My suggestions are generalized enough such that they may be applied according to how the reader sees fit.

Some Notes on Vegetarianism

Notably, I am bringing veganism—rather than vegetarianism—to the fore. I decided to focus on veganism only for the following reasons:

- Veganism is its own category, distinct from vegetarianism.
- Veganism has more negativity attached to it in the eating disorder field because vegans refrain from eating not only animal flesh but also animal by-products. Therefore, veganism is more likely than vegetarianism to be presumed as a form of restriction for the eating disordered person. Great presumption of restriction can lead to a more definitive treatment protocol. For example, many centers don't accommodate vegans but will consider accommodating vegetarians. Since, on the surface, this may seem like the obvious choice, it is more likely to go unchallenged, and therefore, vegans are likely to not get their specific needs met.
- Many vegans are former vegetarians. They may have been vegetarian because they simply were not aware of the connection between animal by-products and the animal industry. For these vegetarians and many others who later make the shift to veganism, the same set of values that influenced their vegetarianism may have also influenced their veganism. Veganism is the one category whose criteria encompasses all categories. It is therefore preferable to understand all points along the vegetarian/vegan spectrum and then adapt this understanding to vegetarians rather than understand vegetarianism without understanding how to adapt it to veganism. If we can understand the ethical issue on the most holistic level possible, then we may better understand its components. And if we can conceptualize a new way of considering and treating vegans, then we can assuredly adapt that framework toward considering and treating vegetarians.
- Various lifestyle and dietary choices are chosen due to ethical values. Vegetarianism may be adopted by one person just as pescetarianism may be adopted by another. If I discussed one, it would seem necessary to discuss them all. For optimal professional impact, I choose to keep this book focused on mainly veganism.
- There is a plethora of existing research about vegetarianism and not very much about veganism on its own. Many of the studies on

vegetarianism group vegetarianism in with pescetarianism and even pollotarians. This research, along with its mainstream presentation, warrants its own separate discussion.

Disclaimers

Throughout this book, I refer to a variety of eating disorder professionals, researchers, and treatment centers in support of my broader point. These references are intended to demonstrate my overall point and are mentioned in specific contexts in which the point is the *idea* rather than the person or organization representing the idea.

This book concerns older adolescents and adults. While I am sure there is room for progress in working with veganism in eating disordered children and younger adolescents, e.g., anyone still growing or anyone who would be on a children's eating disorders unit, I do not explore that here. I do not take any stance on veganism in relation to children or younger adolescents with eating disorders, and I do not apply my ideas to children and younger adolescents. However, while I am not addressing this population specifically, I am also not ruling out the possibility that it can be done. I think that many aspects of the eating disorder field remain in flux and that there is still much to learn and consider.

My experience as a vegan who was not permitted to eat vegan during my own eating disorder treatment has, in part, informed this book. However, I have maintained a healthy detachment from this experience while writing this book. I am connected enough to draw from it authentically but also removed enough to refrain from overidentifying with and generalizing my experience.

In this book, I do not address the concept of adopting veganism as a means of recovering from an eating disorder. This is a topic about which I am less informed, so I cannot speak directly to it. My only stance on it is that I believe in individualized treatment across the board on matters of eating disorders and veganism, and this would include those who adopt veganism as a route to eating disorder recovery.

Lastly, I refer to "clients" and "patients" interchangeably throughout this book.

References

Accanto Health. (n.d.). *The Emily program*. Retrieved April 8, 2022, from www.emilyprogram.com/care-we-offer/frequently-asked-questions/

American Counseling Association. (2014). *2014 ACA code of ethics*. www.counseling.org/docs/default-source/default-document-library/2014-code-of-ethics-finaladdress.pdf

American Psychiatric Association. (2013). *Feeding and eating disorders. Diagnostic and statistical manual of mental disorders* (5th ed., pp. 329–354). American Psychiatric Publishing.

American Psychological Association. (2017). *Ethical principles of psychologists and code of conduct* (2002, amended effective June 1, 2010, and January 1, 2017). www.apa.org/ethics/code/

Brown, A., Fuller, S., & Simic, M. (2019). Consensus statement on considerations for treating vegan patients with eating disorders. *The Royal College of Psychiatrists, The British Dietetic Association and BEAT*. www.rcpsych.ac.uk/docs/default-source/members/faculties/eating-disorders/vegan-patients-eating-disorders-mar19.pdf?sfvrsn=be96d428_2

Fuller, S. J., Brown, A., Rowley, J., & Elliott-Archer, J. (2021). Veganism and eating disorders: Assessment and management considerations. *BJPsych Bulletin, 46*(2), 116–120. https://doi.org/10.1192/bjb.2021.37

National Eating Disorders Association. (n.d.). *Orthorexia*. Retrieved April 5, 2022, from www.nationaleatingdisorders.org/learn/by-eating-disorder/other/orthorexia

Panoff, L. (2020, March 10). Plant-based vs. vegan diet—what's the difference? *Healthline*. Retrieved April 3, 2022, from www.healthline.com/nutrition/plant-based-diet-vs-vegan

Raz, S. (2017). *The vegan's trauma*. (Conference session). The International Association for Relational Psychoanalysis and Psychotherapy.

Root the Future. (2020, November 17). *What is the true definition of 'plant-based' and why does it matter?* Retrieved April 3, 2022, from https://rootthefuture.com/definition-of-plant-based/

The Vegan Society. *Definition of veganism*. www.vegansociety.com/go-vegan/definition-veganism.

Wendel, B. (2019, May 9). *Plant-based diet vs. vegan diet: What's the difference?* Forks Over Knives. Retrieved April 3, 2022, from www.forksoverknives.com/wellness/plant-based-diet-vs-vegan-diet-whats-the-difference/

Section I

ESTABLISHING WHERE WE ARE

In order to go anywhere, we have to know our starting point. This section acknowledges what the current issues are and how they might have taken shape, perhaps unwittingly. I cover my background, my reasons for addressing this subject, and the position from which I approach this text. I relay current perceptions and their various manifestations, introducing a number of voices into the conversation. The issues for vegans with eating disorders are stated and explained clearly throughout the following chapters. Let us now get a lay of the land together . . .

DOI: 10.4324/9781003310617-2

1

MY STORY: EATING DISORDER TREATMENT AND VEGANISM

The topic of eating disorders and veganism is not new, but I hope to—by way of this book—join the voices of those advocating for a shift in its paradigm. In this chapter, I will discuss how my counseling training, eating disorder history, and veganism have informed my current position on the topic of eating disorders and veganism. I hope my explanation presents a holistic picture of my perspectives and envisioned outcomes.

Counseling

I am a therapist. I am currently practicing with a mental health counseling limited permit while working toward licensure. I hold a master's degree in counseling from Goldsmiths, University of London, where I received psychodynamic training. I also hold an advanced mental health counseling certificate from the University at Buffalo, where I gained a cognitive-behavioral and diagnostic psychotherapeutic understanding.

DOI: 10.4324/9781003310617-3

While attending Buffalo's program remotely, I resided and interned in my original home of New York City. My internship site—which later became my place of employment—focused on psychodynamic principles plus a variety of modalities in accordance with clients' needs. I am very happy practicing in this holistic regard. I believe that my psychodynamic foundation informs this book's content and inspires my focus on individualized care.

Eating Disorder

I have recovered from an eating disorder, though it feels odd to say that now because—thanks to this recovery—the eating disorder is no longer a point of reference. That is to say, I no longer view myself in relation to it. It's as though it was a wound that I attended to for a while during recovery. But now the wound has healed. There is scar tissue, but the scar tissue marks a point in time that I now regard with a compassionate neutrality. This neutrality makes it simple for me to discuss my past eating disorder within a vegan context.

Veganism

I am vegan. I became vegan because I formed a connection between an animal's former aliveness and my eating of that animal. It really was as simple as that. For me—for me—it was the obvious choice. I didn't feel special because I suddenly stopped contributing to the harm of animals. Going vegan for me was oddly neutral. I felt lighter in spirit. I felt like I was shedding a layer of something that had never belonged to me. Adopting veganism, in that sense, was about going back to a baseline. The process itself was "something," but once I got there, that was it. I had cut the cord and felt free of my attachment to/incorporation of animals and their by-products (obviously as much as was "practicably possible," which is the well-stated and beautiful point!).

Veganism and Eating Disorders in Treatment

I was in inpatient eating disorder treatment twice: once before I was vegan and once after. In the four years between each treatment stay, I was stable.

Besides being stable, I was myself. I did things that gave me purpose—in particular, making music. I also connected with people—something that my eating disorder had severely deprived me of. I became involved in eating disorder recovery advocacy, performing my music at recovery events and co-organizing an eating disorder conference for family members of eating disordered individuals. During this time, I became vegetarian. Later, upon fully realizing the connection between the dairy and meat industries, I became vegan.

However, in between these two treatment stays, I struggled in ways that were unrelated to food, and these struggles set the stage for a future relapse. My second treatment stay was the result of this relapse. I was required to eat non-vegan food in this treatment setting, which I hold posed a barrier to my recovery.

I remember, even at my sickest, being able to clearly identify my veganism. I remember being acutely aware, during my first meal in treatment, that I was experiencing eating disordered discomfort at biting into a sandwich and vegan discomfort at biting into the piece of chicken inside the sandwich. I never tried to change the menu because I knew prior to admission that this would be required. I did speak to staff about vegan concerns from time to time, and I experienced my veganism as being met with caution. So I mainly focused on eating disorder concerns. For lack of a better term, I "sucked it up." I took a Lactaid tablet before meals containing dairy because I wouldn't have been able to tolerate dairy at this point. One particular night, I got severe stomach cramps after eating too much dairy. This, I figured, was par for the course, a price to pay in recovery. I was uncomfortable consuming non-vegan food throughout the duration of my treatment and began transitioning back to a vegan diet when I left.

After my eating disorder relapse, I headed toward something beyond mere stability: recovery. I got back into eating disorder advocacy. I created and published a book and music project about eating disorders and metaphor. I played music and spoke about recovery at treatment centers, universities, and various recovery events. I attended The New School's Expressive Arts and Health Certificate program, where I learned about a variety of artistic therapeutic techniques and simultaneously evolved in my recovery. I got to know recovery advocates and aligned myself with a recovery mindset. I regularly got out of my own head. I normalized recovery instead of sickness. I connected to spiritual aspects of myself. My relationships strengthened. My connection to animals even strengthened because the "numbness" eating disorder button had gradually been shifted to an off position. I essentially woke up.

Throughout all of this, I maintained that veganism had nothing to do with my eating disorder. For me—for me—consciously acknowledging animals' sentience to the extent that I had to refrain from consuming them was nowhere near my eating disordered mindset. I'm talking about two different pathways that had no bearing whatsoever on each other. Trying to imagine it is baffling. These were separate journeys. They wouldn't have come into contact with one another if not for my eating disorder treatment—which, by the way, I understand. I am not blaming my treatment team. Veganism was just getting on the map at the time, but the truth still stands that eating disorder treatment was the only place where my eating disorder and my veganism ever had anything to do with one another.

Preceding and during this relapse, I was seeing an outpatient dietitian and a therapist who never pressured me to change my vegan decision. With them, there was always an understanding that veganism was not the problem and that my choosing veganism, in and of itself, did not contribute to my eating disorder. There was an understanding that, going forward, I would not be at risk of restricting due to my veganism. Eating disordered thought and behavior discussions were always focused on my actual issues, which I sincerely appreciated.

However, my story is just my own. There are many people with eating disorders for whom veganism truly is the eating disordered guise that my inpatient treatment team had asked about or for whom veganism may be unsustainable in recovery, which my treatment team had cautioned me of. Their stories carry equal weight in this discussion. There are also many ethical vegans who either struggle more than I struggled or don't go to treatment to begin with because of the lack of vegan options. Their stories also carry equal weight. Every eating disordered and vegan-identifying person's story is equal in value. The point of this book is to raise the level of those ethical vegans to the same level of those whose veganism is not authentic and thus will do a disservice to their recovery. There is an inherent risk in failing to clarify and conceptualize veganism in the eating disorder field as well as an inherent risk in neglecting to recognize the breadth of a vegan's experience.

Two Communities

I recognize that I am positioned in two communities—the vegan community and the eating disorder community. Rather than attempting to toe a line throughout this book, I want to speak genuinely from my position within both. From this position, I want to show that one community's philosophy need not negate the other's. As you will see, I have not taken a hard stance on the topic of eating disorders and veganism from the perspective of either community. My veganism informs my perspective on vegans just as my eating disordered history informs my perspective on eating disorders. Most importantly, however, my counseling training informs my perspective on the treatment of clients.

As such, my response to any question from either community will invariably be based on the need to support vegan eating disorder patients. Because I do not know these specific patients, I cannot form conclusions derived from personal experience as a vegan or as a recovered eating disordered individual, nor can I let my connection to either of these categories inform my vision of what recovery looks like for any given person. I recognize that it is not my place to prioritize ideas over eating disordered patients themselves. What I can prioritize, however, are the counseling principles that would apply to any topic, this being one of them. My counseling experience thus informs my aim to adopt openness, curiosity, and neutrality. My only solid stance in this book is that we need to start from an open, curious, and neutral space. Because starting from this space will end up meaning different things for different vegan patients— including those who think they are vegan only to realize that "veganism" was a sneaky little label that their eating disorder concocted—then there is no stance to take beyond it.

So, hi, vegan community, I see you there, you amazingly lovely and wonderful vegan advocates and friends. And no, I will not be advocating for following a vegan diet as the solution for all eating disorder patients identifying as vegan. Also, hi, eating disorder field people! You lovely, amazing people who help people like me go from sickness to recovery. We've worked together, I've sung on stages with you, I've lobbied with you, I adore the heck out of you! *And* I will be challenging the accepted consensus that "veganism-is-restrictive-therefore-veganism-bad." I'm with you, and I'm also speaking to you. We need to work on this. It's about time.

2

AN UNCOMFORTABLE TASK AHEAD

The eating disorder field is being presented with the challenge of creating a shift in how vegan clients with eating disorders are perceived, supported, and treated. The field is positioned to reevaluate its current stance on vegan eating disordered individuals' potential for recovery and subsequent professional approaches.

In 2019, an informal survey of 100 eating disorder registered dietitians taken through the International Federation of Eating Disorder Dietitians list serve revealed that 98 percent of dietitians working in the eating disorder field (most practicing for over ten years) had worked with eating disordered clients who followed a vegan lifestyle (T. Beasley, personal communication, March 23, 2022). Survey results showed that the clients of these dietitians needed a higher level of care than their current weekly outpatient treatment sessions, but because clients expressed a need for vegan treatment, the lack of vegan-accommodating treatment centers presented a challenge in getting clients the care they needed. The

DOI: 10.4324/9781003310617-4

dietitians thus felt stuck toeing the line between providing care at a level of treatment that was insufficient for these clients' needs, while trying to find them a higher level of care that would treat them as vegans.

A qualitative Danish study consisting of 18 women who had declined eating disorder treatment found that, among other reasons, those

> "refusing treatment may prefer: a focus on emotional and psychological wellbeing more than on weight gain and ED symptoms, to become active agents engaged in their own treatment and to receive support that promotes their personal responsibility and agency, acknowledgement of individual differences and tailored interventions to patient's self-identified needs, a therapist who listens to the patient's perspective, [and] a therapist who sees the 'whole person' instead of only focusing on the ED"

(Andersen et al., 2021, p. 10). While veganism was not a part of this study, the preferences represent treatment's limitations in relation to vegan clients. As seen throughout this book, vegan eating disorder sufferers may decline treatment or experience unnecessary pain during it due to unfulfilled vegan-specific needs. The vegan-informed approach, which is the culmination of this book, emphasizes the need to acknowledge a vegan eating disordered person's agency, listen openly to the vegan's perspective, and regard the vegan as a whole person. It would make sense, then, that a vegan might avoid seeking treatment if their needs in these areas fell short.

According to Brown et al. (2019, p. 3), "Treating someone with anorexia nervosa requires respecting that person's religion or beliefs, including veganism, while ensuring that they are not discriminated against in terms of the quality of treatment they receive." While also acknowledging that "using products derived from animals may be necessary under certain circumstances," they emphasize that—barring necessary exceptions—a vegan diet in treatment can be achieved. In conjunction with this knowledge, some eating disorder facilities have begun providing vegan care, such as Alsana, BALANCE Eating Disorder Treatment Center™, The Emily Program and Veritas Collaborative, and others. I hope to contribute to this growing movement, which I will refer to throughout this book as "vegan-informed" treatment. Thanks to those who are already implementing vegan-related principles into treatment, the movement has already begun.

It is understandable to consider turning someone away from treatment if they are likely to engage in certain treatment-interfering behaviors, as these behaviors may present harm to themselves and likely others (discussed in Chapter 4). However, I will speculate here that it seems as though vegans are not being admitted to treatment on the premise that vegan eating, for eating disordered individuals, is itself treatment-interfering. I will speculate further that the lack of admission to treatment may be viewed by professionals as a lack of recovery readiness (as "evidenced" by the refusal to forgo their vegan eating, read: let go of attachment to their eating disordered behaviors). However, we need to acknowledge that *anything* presenting possible damage to patients is treatment interfering, *including* when a vegan person—just as a non-vegan person—is restricting their food.

Every time we think of the word "vegan," let us associate it with "an ethical commitment to not harming or exploiting animals." The idea is to associate "veganism" with words like these instead of eating disorder words. Furthermore, any eating disorder symptoms that are disguised under the term "veganism" need to be viewed simply as eating disorder symptoms. And from this perspective, we can view the problem more clearly.

There are three vital pieces of information that make it essential to reassess the attitude to veganism and eating disorders:

- Many vegan eating disordered clients are not going to treatment at the critical point when treatment is needed.
- Many vegan eating disordered clients who do go to non-vegan treatment when higher levels of care are needed find themselves in an inherently compromised position, which can make it harder for them to participate in treatment, receive appropriate support, and ultimately reach recovery by way of the treatment.
- Eating disorders are on the rise (Rafferty, 2021; The American Journal of Clinical Nutrition, 2019, p. 1402), and even more since the start of the pandemic (Rafferty, 2021; Katella, 2021; Termorshuizen et al., 2020, p. 1780). Additionally, an increasing number of people are becoming vegan (The Vegan Society). This is the reality we are facing. Positive recovery outcomes are higher for eating disordered

individuals who begin treatment early (Jones & Brown, n.d.). It is reasonable, then, to posit that the issue of veganism, eating disorders, and treatment will subsist and, as such, that there is a need for treatment to adapt accordingly. Importantly, we should recognize the rise of both eating disorders and veganism while also refraining from assuming causation. Blogger Olivia Rafferty (2021) acknowledges the rise of both veganism and eating disorders in the UK, taking care to mention that the dual rise "shouldn't be treated as a case of causation" and that "the two are very separate entities—simply two parallel lines pointing upwards, never necessarily touching."

These three points lead me to speculate that non-ethically-based vegans are likely overrepresented in accounts of clinical experience with eating disordered patients. Since these individuals don't have an ethical belief in their veganism and are instead following it for dietary reasons, the non-vegan aspect of treatment alone might not markedly interfere with their treatment pursuits. Ethical vegans, on the other hand, may not consider eating disorder treatment because they couldn't bear the thought of partaking in animal mistreatment or consumption. If we consider that those ethical vegans who do go to treatment have done so because they feel there is no option left, we can begin to imagine how difficult it might be for them. That difficulty is compounded by professional assumptions that they represent a minority of eating disorder patients, when in reality it is possible that the vegan majority are not receiving the treatment they need and are thus underrepresented in clinical accounts.

The field can support vegan eating disordered individuals by bringing previously unconsidered vegan-related concerns to the fore. Only then will all clients who say they are vegan (rather than just those whose proclaimed veganism is an eating disordered guise) will have a chance of their needs being met in treatment. Making space to fully consider a vegan patient's needs does not take away from considering the needs of a patient who falsely claims veganism. But we need to have both at the ready—the consideration that it *may not* be true veganism and the consideration that it *may* be true veganism.

These are starting points. That said, the solution is not clear-cut. As you will see throughout this book, I argue in favor of nuance again and again, but we cannot fathom reaching a viable solution for any patient—regardless of their circumstance—without a clearly identifiable problem. The problem is that the vegan-specific needs of vegan eating disordered patients are not being considered. The problem serves as a solid baseline to which we can refer anytime we get lost in the search for a solution. No matter how fuzzy the solution may seem, we can at least have a shared conceptualization of the problem. We can at least point to this identifiable knowledge and ask ourselves, "What now?"

References

Alsana Home. *Alsana®*. Retrieved April 3, 2022, from www.alsana.com/

Andersen, S. T., Linkhorst, T., Gildberg, F. A., & Sjögren, M. (2021). Why do women with eating disorders decline treatment? A qualitative study of barriers to specialized eating disorder treatment. *Nutrients, 13*(11), 4033. https://doi.org/10.3390/nu13114033

BALANCE Eating Disorder Treatment Center™. (n.d.). Retrieved April 3, 2022, from https://balancedtx.com/

Brown, A., Fuller, S., & Simic, M. (2019). *Consensus statement on considerations for treating vegan patients with eating disorders.* The Royal College of Psychiatrists, The British Dietetic Association and BEAT. www.rcpsych.ac.uk/docs/default-source/members/faculties/eating-disorders/vegan-patients-eating-disorders-mar19.pdf?sfvrsn=be96d428_2

Jones, M., & Brown, T. (n.d.). *Why early intervention for eating disorders is essential.* Retrieved April 5, 2022, from www.nationaleatingdisorders.org/blog/why-early-intervention-eating-disorders-essential

Katella, K. (2021, June 15). Eating disorders on the rise after our pandemic year. *Yale Medicine.* Retrieved April 3, 2022, from www.yalemedicine.org/news/eating-disorders-pandemic

Rafferty, O. (2021, February 25). Breaking food rules with veganism. *The Vegan Review.* Retrieved April 3, 2022, from https://theveganreview.com/breaking-food-rules-veganism-eating-disorders/

Termorshuizen, J. D., Watson, H. J., Thornton, L. M., Borg, S., Flatt, R. E., MacDermod, C. M., Harper, L. E., van Furth, E. F., Peat, C. M., & Bulik, C. M. (2020). Early impact of COVID-19 on individuals with self-reported eating disorders: A survey of ~1,000 individuals in the United States and the Netherlands. *The International Journal of Eating Disorders, 53*(11), 1780–1790. https://doi.org/10.1002/eat.23353

The Emily Program. (2021, March 23). *The Emily program and veritas collaborative are joining forces to expand care*. Retrieved April 3, 2022, from www.emilyprogram.com/blog/the-emily-program-and-veritas-collaborative-are-joining-forces-to-expand-care/

The Vegan Society. *Definition of veganism*. www.vegansociety.com/go-vegan/definition-veganism.

3

PUBLIC PERCEPTION AT A GLANCE

In this chapter, I will demonstrate how negative perceptions of eating disorders and veganism are often presented in public spheres. This demonstration will allow us to plainly reference current perspectives on eating disorders and veganism. Let us consider this overview an outermost measure of where we are at baseline and a subsequent indicator of where to go next.

A Widely Mentioned Eating Disorder Indicator

Negative depictions of veganism as a potential eating disorder indicator exist across a plethora of websites. I have reviewed how a range of varied websites presents veganism alongside eating disorders. The websites—consisting of those representing eating disorder treatment facilities, eating disorder resource organizations, eating disorder family support organizations, a health and wellness center, a university, a public school

DOI: 10.4324/9781003310617-5

district, and two magazines—cite (almost exclusively) a singular phrase intended to indicate a possible eating disorder sign. The phrase is: "any new practice with food or fad diets, including cutting out entire food groups (no sugar, no carbs, no dairy, *vegetarianism/veganism)." It originates on The National Eating Disorders Association (NEDA)'s website under "Emotional and Behavioral Signs of an Eating Disorder," a list that follows NEDA's statement that

> those struggling with an eating disorder may have some, but not all, of the following emotional and behavioral signs. Presence of any of the signs that your loved one may be struggling is cause for serious concern and you should encourage them to seek professional help.
> (National Eating Disorders Association, n.d.)

In the following discussion, I will highlight each website's use of NEDA's phrase, how certain websites applied NEDA's phrase to some eating disorder diagnoses and not to other eating disorder diagnoses, and how the application of this phrase differed across websites.

As subtle as veganism's inclusion here might seem, identifying it is important. In fact, the ease with which one can simply see it and move along speaks to the need to address veganism in this context. "Veganism" is not a word that haphazardly belongs alongside "no sugar, no carbs, no dairy," because those describe primarily dietary practices and, as per the definitions highlighted in this book's introduction, veganism is not a diet at its core. I can imagine some saying that the inclusion of this one word—heck, a mere example of a larger point—is not worth a deep dive. To that hypothetical wondering, I will preemptively respond that the extent to which its inclusion and subsequent reception is seamless is the extent to which it ought to be discussed. After all, the point of this book is to build a pause between a view's espousal and subsequent adoption. In that pause, there needs to be analysis. So . . . shall we?

First, let us focus on the inconsistent application of the phrase, as seen in the following examples:

- The National Eating Disorders Association (Nationaleatingdisorders.org), which authored the phrase, is inconsistent about it across its website. It lists veganism as an indicator for eating disorders in general, but on the NEDA website's individual pages, it lists veganism under binge eating disorder, OSFED, and orthorexia—orthorexia phrased as "cutting out an increasing number of food groups (all sugar, all carbs, all dairy, all meat, all animal products)"—but omits it for anorexia and bulimia.

- Anxiety and Depression Association of America (ADAA.org), an educational and resourceful organization, lists it under eating disorders in general.
- The University of North Carolina, Wilmington (UNCW.edu), lists it under eating concerns in general on their website's Counseling page. (UNCW does not have any conflicting diagnostic categories.)
- Family Caregiver Support (Family-caregiver-support.eu), a European caregiver organization, lists it under eating disorders in general—in its introduction to the list notably adding the words, "most common symptoms." (Family Caregiver Support does not have any conflicting diagnostic categories.)
- Cypress Magazine (Cypressmag.com), a magazine that covers a variety of content in connection with West Tennessee, lists it under eating disorders in general for Eating Disorder Awareness Week 2019 (Cypress Magazine does not have any conflicting diagnostic categories).
- Barrington Behavioral Health and Wellness (BarringtonBHW.com), a service providing mental health treatment at various Illinois locations, lists it under eating disorders in general for Eating Disorders Awareness Week 2017 (Barrington BHW does not have any conflicting diagnostic categories).
- Eating Disorder Hope (EatingDisorderHope.com), an informative and resourceful eating disorder website, lists it under OSFED but omits it for anorexia, bulimia, binge eating disorder, and orthorexia.
- Seeds of Hope (SeedsofHope.pyramidhealthcarepa.com), an outpatient eating disorder treatment clinic with multiple locations in Southeastern Pennsylvania, lists it under binge eating disorder, bulimia, and OSFED but omits it for anorexia.
- Alaska Eating Disorders Alliance (AKeatingdisordersalliance.org), a resource providing support, advocacy, and education, includes it

for bulimia, binge eating disorder, OSFED, and orthorexia—listed as "cutting out an increasing number of food groups (all sugar, all carbs, all dairy, all meat, all animal products)"—and omits it for anorexia.

- Fairhaven Treatment Center (Fairhaventc.com), lists it under binge eating disorder and OSFED but omits it under anorexia and bulimia.
- Multi-Service Eating Disorders Association (Medainc.org), an educational and advocacy resource, lists it under OSFED but omits it under anorexia, bulimia, and binge eating disorder.
- The Livermore, California school district website (LivermoreSchools. org) omits it under anorexia, bulimia, and binge eating disorder.
- Center for Discovery (Centerfordiscovery.com), an eating disorder treatment center, lists "Veganism, Vegetarian or Pescetarian" under "Symptoms & Warning Signs" of orthorexia but omits it for anorexia, bulimia, binge eating disorder, and OSFED.

From this sample, we may infer that veganism is a possible eating disorder indicator regarding:

- Eating disorders in general, according to NEDA, Anxiety and Depression Association of America, University of North Carolina Wilmington Counseling, Cypress Magazine, and Barrington Behavioral Health and Wellness
- OSFED, according to NEDA, Eating Disorder Hope, Seeds of Hope, Alaska Eating Disorders Alliance, Fairhaven Treatment Center, and MEDA.
- Binge Eating Disorder, according to NEDA, Seeds of Hope, Alaska Eating Disorders Alliance, and Fairhaven Treatment Center.
- Bulimia, according to Seeds of Hope and Alaska Eating Disorders Alliance.
- Orthorexia, according to NEDA, Alaska Eating Disorders Alliance, and Center for Discovery.

On the flip side, veganism is purportedly not an eating disorder indicator regarding:

- Binge eating disorder, according to Eating Disorder Hope, Livermore Schools, MEDA, and Center for Discovery.
- Bulimia, according to a page on NEDA's website (listing the indicator under "eating disorders in general" but not under "Bulimia"), Eating Disorder Hope, Livermore Schools, Fairhaven Treatment Center, MEDA, and Center for Discovery.
- Anorexia, according to NEDA (listing the indicator under "eating disorders in general" but not under "Anorexia"), Eating Disorder Hope, Seeds of Hope, Alaska Eating Disorders Alliance, Livermore Schools, Fairhaven Treatment Center, MEDA, and Center for Discovery—in other words, every website that had a category for anorexia.
- Orthorexia, according to Eating Disorder Hope.
- OSFED, according to Center for Discovery.

Additionally, NEDA listed veganism as a general sign for eating disorders while also omitting it from certain categories on other parts of its website. This inconsistency might further confuse readers of NEDA's website. Since the phrase originated from NEDA, any site which included veganism as a "general" eating disorder sign without also specifying its potential for omission risks further misleading readers.

Interestingly, many websites name veganism as a possible indicator of eating disorders but not in the category of anorexia. Given the widespread perception that veganism is restrictive and therefore should not be practiced in eating disorder recovery, I would be remiss to neglect the notable absence of this prospective warning sign from the category of anorexia. After all, restriction is the eating disorder behavior most closely associated with veganism in the eating disorder field, and restriction is particularly associated with anorexia. If its absence is *unintentional*, then readers are not being presented with all of the information that the article aims to present. If its absence is *intentional*, then readers are being presented with a logical fallacy without explanation. Either way, information is missing.

Moreover, with a single exception, the phrase is universally listed under OSFED. Since the diagnosis of OSFED inherently recognizes gray areas, it is worth recognizing the gray area inherent to discussions of veganism and eating disorders.

The widespread and varied nature of veganism's possible indication of an eating disorder warning sign conflates the line between eating disorders and veganism. Families are receiving information about eating disorders to help a loved one, perhaps for the first time. Students are learning this information as a part of their curricula. Additionally, due to inconsistent distribution of the phrase, people reading one source are being informed that veganism is a sign of a particular type of eating disorder, while people reading a different source are not. Is it not a far cry, then, to surmise that veganism's broad and inconsistent application as a warning sign of an eating disorder increases misconceptions about veganism's association with eating disorders to the general public? This is concerning because sites that intend to educate the general public about eating disorders are often the first stop for many in their search for information.

Many sources conflate veganism and eating disorders. I have highlighted a sample of mixed and potentially misleading messages across organizations and even within an organization (NEDA) itself. The apparent association between the two concepts is so prevalent—and the subsequent takeaway so automatic—that many people may not stop to question it. A quick survey of internet sources indicates veganism's collectively agreed-upon cautionary status. This automatic perception can leak into and dually influence both general and professional perception on the topic.

*Vegetarianism's inclusion is important as well, but that lends itself to a separate discussion that would digress from the point of this book.

References

Alaska Eating Disorders Alliance. *Binge eating disorder.* www.akeatingdisordersalliance.org/binge-eating-disorder

Alaska Eating Disorders Alliance. *Bulimia nervosa.* www.akeatingdisordersalliance.org/bulimia-nervosa

Alaska Eating Disorders Alliance. *OSFED.* www.akeatingdisordersalliance.org/other-specified-feeding-or-eating-d

Barrington Behavioral Health & Wellness. (2017, February 28). *Eating disorder awareness week 2017.* www.barringtonbhw.com/eating-disorder-awareness-week-2017/

Center for Discovery. *Orthorexia nervosa signs and symptoms*. https://centerfordiscovery.com/conditions/orthorexia/

Counseling Center. *Body image & eating concerns*. University of North Carolina Wilmington. https://uncw.edu/counseling/bodyimageandeatingconcerns.html#Body%20Image

Eating Disorders | Anxiety and Depression Association of America, ADAA. (n.d.). *Eating disorders*. Retrieved April 6, 2022, from https://adaa.org/understanding-anxiety/co-occurring-disorders/eating-disorders#Signs%20and%20Symptoms

Eating Disorder Hope. (2019, December 11). *Defining other specified feeding and eating disorder OSFED*. www.eatingdisorderhope.com/blog/osfed-defining-other-specified-feeding-eating-disorder.

Fairhaven Treatment Center. (2019, February 18). *What we treat*. www.fairhaventc.com/what-we-treat/.

Family Caregiver Support. *Module 5: Eating disorders*. www.family-caregiver-support.eu/wp-content/uploads/2020/01/M5-Eating-disorders-EN.pdfIt's eating disorder awareness week. *Cypress Magazine Blog*. www.cypressmag.com/blog/2018/2/9/its-eating-disorder-awareness-week?rq=eating%20disorder%20awareness%20week

Mental Health/Eating Disorders. www.livermoreschools.org/Page/8064.

Multi-Service Eating Disorders Association. (2019, January 10). *About eating disorders*. www.medainc.org/resources-2/about-eating-disorders/.

National Eating Disorders Association. (n.d.). *Emotional and behavioral signs of an eating disorder*. Retrieved April 15, 2022, from www.nationaleatingdisorders.org/toolkit/parent-toolkit/emotional-behavioral-signs

Seeds of Hope. (2020, December 1). *Binge eating disorder*. https://seedsofhope.pyramidhealthcarepa.com/education-center/binge-eating-disorder/.

Seeds of Hope. (2021a, January 21). *Bulimia signs and symptoms*. https://seedsofhope.pyramidhealthcarepa.com/education-center/bulimia/.

Seeds of Hope. (2021b, January 21). *Other specified feeding or eating disorders*. https://seedsofhope.pyramidhealthcarepa.com/education-center/osfed/.

4

RECOVERY PERSPECTIVES

If we believe that veganism is an eating disorder warning sign, we may apply that belief to professional recovery perspectives. This chapter will explore various perceptions of eating disorders and veganism within the eating disorder field and subsequent professional connotations. It will take a deeper look at the misconceptions highlighted in the previous chapter. The previous chapter surveyed the land; this chapter will dig deeper.

I will start by highlighting some fundamental differences between eating disordered restriction and the dietary component of veganism.

Professional Outcomes of Misconceptions

Understandably, when treatment providers are presented with eating disordered patients claiming to be on certain self-imposed diets, they would aim to deter these patients from their diet mentality. However, if providers mistake veganism for a diet rather than an ethical stance, they risk providing misguided treatment. This is important to acknowledge because veganism is not something to be treated. While, of course, there are those who abstain from eating animal products for dietary purposes, choosing to do so for ethical reasons is the defining marker of veganism; therefore, veganism does not inherently connote restriction. There is nothing inherently about veganism that would make a person restrict their food intake. Indeed, when I spoke to a former eating disorder patient, Emily, she said,

> There is this assumption that veganism is restrictive and while I do wholeheartedly acknowledge that it could be for some (if they are plant-based and not ethically vegan), that is such a general assumption that totally dismisses ethical vegans who wish to not contribute to animal exploitation, suffering, commodification, and do not view animal products as food for that matter.
>
> (Emily, personal communication, March 12, 2022)

Selecting Versus Restricting, Incorporating Versus Omitting

The eating disordered mindset understandably cannot be trusted. It certainly cannot be trusted to know what is best for the eating disordered person. It is therefore thought that eating disordered individuals, to a certain extent, may lack agency. Eating disordered individuals might think they are making decisions on their own behalf, in accordance with their own logic, when in fact, it is really their eating disorder that is making the decision for them. It follows that, when eating disordered individuals adopt the label of "veganism" as a restrictive guise, they are not *choosing* the vegan food so much as they are *refraining* from choosing something else. They are not making a conscious, deliberate *selection*; instead, they are making an unconscious, anxiety-driven *omission* of everything but the vegan food. "What *can't* I have?" an eating disordered person might ask themselves. Veganism, on the other hand, is a conscious process of intentionally *selecting*—not *restricting*—food. Vegans, in *selecting* food, are *invoking* their agency via their ethical beliefs. Vegans focus on *incorporating* vegan food into their lives. They gravitate toward what they *can* eat. By contrast, an eating disordered person falsely claiming veganism does not invoke ethics into their eating disordered restriction, even if that restriction involves eating vegan food.

Closed Versus Open

Let us now look at eating disorders and veganism through a closed-versus-open lens, respectively. Eating disordered individuals with restrictive behaviors adopt *closed* stances on food. They work within—and abide by—eating-disorder-imposed limitations, no matter the cost to their well-being. Vegan individuals, on the other hand, adopt *open* stances on food. They operate within a boundary determined by a value system. By extension, they are not stuck within any presupposed limitation. Instead, they are compelled to expand their attitude toward trying new foods.

The natural response to vegans' perception of limited choices is to find *more* choices, not to stay confined within these boundaries to a fault, like the eating disordered person would. Most importantly, they would do whatever was "possible and practicable" (in line with the definition of veganism) to act according to their vegan values. They would become resourceful, ask questions, and learn. They would feel positive about the extent of possible foods available to them. They would naturally seek out *more* knowledge and *more* sources of sustenance in an expansive manner.

A vegan's values do not keep the vegan stuck; instead, they propel the vegan to become *more* conscious, *more* aware, *more* present. The restrictive eating disordered mentality, by contrast, is *less* conscious, *less* aware, *less* present. Restrictive eating disordered behaviors are motivated by anxiety and fear, by figuring out the *least bad* option. Vegan decisions, on the other hand, are based on finding the *most preferable* option.

Veganism and Diet

A common misconception about veganism is that it is one and the same as some particular way of eating. An example of this might be eating a raw vegan diet—as though raw veganism were an inherent branch of veganism. In reality, eating raw can be a way of eating vegan, but eating vegan does not necessitate eating raw. A raw vegan person may be vegan due to ethical concerns, but—because rawness alone has no bearing on animal treatment—eating raw food is not an essential component of veganism. Linking veganism to raw eating thus perpetuates the misguided association between veganism and restriction.

The "alternative food network" pertains (in part) to "niche food not produced by the conventional system" (Goodman & Goodman, 2007). When inclined to equate rawness to veganism, we should consider a 2016 study by Barnett et al., which found that alternative food network tendencies "were associated with less disordered eating," thereby challenging

> the idea that the 'food rules' espoused by the AFN prompt the development of restrictive, disordered eating behaviors as well as the notion that individuals already suffering from disordered eating behaviors use the 'food rules' put forth by the AFN as convenient categories to regulate and restrict consumption.
>
> (p. 718)

Brytek-Matera et al. (2018) include veganism as a "special diet" among subcategories of "pescatarian, . . . paleo, gluten-free and raw diet." They also claim that "the higher incidence of eating disorders relating to vegetarianism suggests that special diets may be connected to disordered eating behaviours and serve as socially acceptable means to mask disordered eating behaviours." They go on to include veganism among "vegetarian, fruitarian, and raw food diet[s]" in their association between "following specific diets or food rules" and "dietary patterns" (p. 442). It therefore makes sense that their findings would be "in line with the results of the latest research, which have shown that vegetarians and vegans do not differ in orthorexic eating behaviour, but both groups presented higher levels of orthorexic eating behaviour than individuals with rare and frequent meat consumption" (p. 449).

Professional Implications of Misconstruing Veganism with Dietary Restriction

Having discussed some fundamental differences between eating disordered restriction and the dietary component of veganism, I will now discuss why this knowledge is important for providing beneficial eating disorder treatment to vegan patients.

Generally, effective eating disorder treatment acknowledges that the type of diet a patient follows is considered secondarily to the fact that there is a diet at all. Whether this diet is keto, paleo, raw, etc., food is still very much the focus of the disorder. Kofsky (2020) takes care to distinguish that "those who follow ketogenic, Whole 30, [and] paleo, are also vulnerable to disordered eating habits. Any type of 'diet' that eliminates food groups leaves a person susceptible to an eating disorder." Blogger Jasmine Briones says,

> I used vegan as an excuse to hide my poor eating habits in social situations . . . eventually, once I read books, watched documentaries, and spoke with others who had also adopted a plant-based diet, I properly understood and executed a plant-based diet and learned about the ethical treatment of animals, the effect of factory farming on the environment etc., and went vegan for all of the reasons I am vegan today.
>
> (Briones, 2019)

For an eating disordered person who is restricting, eating vegan food can be a restrictive approach, but then, by that logic, anything that Kofsky mentioned can be as well.

Eating Disorder Non-Negotiables

Professionally held perspectives influence treatment protocol. An important aspect of eating disorder treatment protocol is "non-negotiables"—or treatment "boundaries"—as outlined in the Eating Disorder Services guidelines for British Columbia. According to Geller et al. (2012, pp. 14–15), implementing treatment non-negotiables involves "having a sound rationale for treatment non-negotiables, . . . providing ample advance warning of treatment expectations, . . . implementing boundaries consistently . . . and maximizing patient autonomy." These non-negotiables serve to protect all patients.

Non-negotiables make sense in treatment, so, by extension, restriction as a non-negotiable fits the bill. Surely, restriction and recovery conflict with each other? It would therefore be reprehensible to encourage restriction as a part of recovery; certainly, deeming it *integral* to recovery would be preposterous! Encouraging restriction would unequivocally cause harm, ultimately permitting the eating disorder to take the reins. "Hallelujah," the eating disorder would say. "I've just been given the green light!" Restriction, therefore, absolutely is a treatment non-negotiable. Consequently, if a patient restricts during a meal, protocol might entail, for example, drinking a nutritional supplement to compensate for missed calories or decreasing previously permitted physical activity to prevent burning excess calories. Such consequences might, at times, be perceived by the patients as punishments. Professionals would attribute this perception to the eating disordered mentality—surely, a person who isn't in the grips of an eating disorder can logically understand this consequential reasoning? But a person wrapped up in an eating disorder might have a hard time recognizing and/or accepting that this consequence is intended to help them.

Since veganism is often regarded as a form of restriction, it too might be considered a non-negotiable—a determination justified with the same reasoning as other non-negotiables: namely, that it is damaging to patients. Believing that veganism equates to food restriction certainly seems to justify the conclusion that veganism is bad for recovery. Properly addressing veganism's non-negotiable status for vegan eating disordered individuals necessitates examination of such professional assumptions. The rationale for deeming veganism as a non-negotiable must be thoroughly assessed. This assessment would begin by confirming the fundamental distinctions between veganism and eating disorders.

Alsana, the first eating disorder treatment center to offer fully vegan treatment to its vegan clients, makes this distinction clear. Tammy Beasley, MS, RDN, CEDS-S, LD, who served as Alsana's VP of clinical nutrition services during the years Alsana developed and implemented its vegan programming and is now the national strategic advisor for Nutrition Outreach and Education at Integrative Life Network, says, "Practicing vegans can have eating disorders, but veganism itself isn't one" (Beasley, 2020). Alsana therefore assumes a "responsibility to learn about the difference between veganism and restriction, or veganism and orthorexia, so [they] can be an advocate for [their] vegan clients to help them discover this too."

Ultimately, a vegan person's recovery goal would be attaining freedom from fear and any other unhealthy psychological attachment to food, just the same as any other patient. Therefore, a recovery goal for an ethical vegan would be an ability to eat all kinds of vegan food where none of it is off-limits.

Veganism as a Trigger

When I talk about eating disorder triggers in mental health settings, I am referring to eating disordered actions or comments that negatively impact other patients. Different patients consider different mealtime content triggering, and beyond that, different patients react differently to potentially triggering content. For the purposes of this discussion, anything can be a trigger when patients sit at a table together. In my experience as a patient, I have seen people hiding their food; people receiving more food than their meal plan had indicated; and people eating different meals from others in accordance with their treatment requirements. Patients could potentially feel triggered by any of these scenarios. Everyone is going through their own process, and it is therefore important to focus on one's own recovery. Refraining from comparing food is one way of refraining from comparing one's own recovery to another's recovery.

Treatment provides the space in which to safely experience a triggering feeling and process the emotions that might arise in the absence of a maladaptive coping mechanism. If, for example, someone takes issue with someone else eating a meal that differs from their own, their reaction can be considered an opportunity to discuss their feelings about it in therapy.

On the premise of this understanding, let us consider the oft-presumed risk to other patients when a patient is allowed to have a vegan meal. Because, as previously discussed, veganism is often taken for restriction, the overarching concern is that patients will feel triggered by someone getting to restrict while they cannot; getting to choose certain foods while they cannot; getting to have a different, perhaps "special," meal catered just to them, while they, again, cannot. Certainly, avoiding triggers is key to effective treatment, and therefore measures are taken to ensure the absence of unnecessary triggers where possible. Like treatment non-negotiables, we see these measures enacted at the table.

I recognize this concern and have been on the receiving end of it. In my treatment experience, it was assumed that all patients would typically eat the same food as one another at mealtimes. While it was rare that any two meals would be identical (due to different caloric requirements and different stages of treatment), a certain homogeneity was implied.

It is understandable, then, that getting what is perceived to be a "special meal" might derail the whole message of treatment. It would naturally follow that veering from the recommended homogeneity is detrimental to all patients.

I believe that treatment should safely incorporate vegan matters. I advocate for a collective acknowledgment that in eating disorder treatment, every patient's treatment plan must be inherently challenging. Therefore, vegans, while perhaps getting a different meal than their fellow patients, are still not at any more of an advantage for the simple reason that their meal is not what their eating disorder would choose. Just like patients who are kosher and patients who have food allergies, vegan eating disorder patients would likely not have chosen treatment-provided meals of their own volition—hence why they are in treatment in the first place.

At its core, this concern is not about veganism. Rather, it is about a vegan person's consumption of something *different*. As I will discuss in Chapter 6, vegan eating disorder patients are not eating food that they prefer to eat; they are not given a pass to eat their "safe" foods only. They are simply *not* eating non-vegan food—a preference warranted by an ethical philosophy rather than an eating disordered fear. In the absence of further context, refraining from serving a vegan patient non-vegan food does not assuage an eating disordered fear.

Neglecting to realize this fact can end up impacting both vegans and non-vegans during mealtimes. This impact can blur into other aspects of treatment as well, such as therapy groups consisting of both vegans and non-vegans. If unaddressed, vegan content arising within these groups may elicit unsettling emotions that facilitators who are not informed about veganism may feel unequipped to navigate. Since intense emotions in eating disorder treatment can latch onto anything in their purview, it is important that professionals feel equipped to help all patients, including vegans, vegetarians, non-vegans, etc. Group facilitators need to hold each person's experience in full while navigating interpersonal communication between group members. This may mean that professionals help non-vegan patients sort through the ways in which their eating disorder may be filtering vegan content through a distorted lens.

There is also room to consider that a vegan patient may feel upset by fellow patients eating animals and their by-products, especially since this food is not only normalized but also synonymized with attaining recovery (discussed further in Chapter 8). Because vegan-specific professional considerations are still in their early stages, it is not fair to assume that a vegan person can walk into treatment knowing how to navigate this situation. A normalized system of animal consumption surrounds them. In these settings, non-vegan-eating is presumed. The vegan patient cannot assume that their treatment providers will understand their vegan concerns. Hence, they may feel isolated, overlooked, and misunderstood. Such a struggle is not a natural part of recovery. However, the onus is on the vegan to adapt to the majority rather than on the majority to understand of the vegan (discussed further in Chapter 15). Vegan psychologist and author Clare Mann, BSc (Hons), MSc, MA, Post Grad Dip. COcc Psychol. AMAPS, FBPS, UKCP, found in a 2018 survey that "the biggest challenge for vegans was being around others eating animal products" (2018, p. 49).

Treatment Centers' Non-Acceptance of Vegans

As a result of this rationale on veganism and restriction, treatment centers often-times do not accept vegan patients. This is a pivotal point of discussion because eating disordered individuals cannot afford to lose time in pursuing treatment.

Time is lost for several reasons when a patient is turned away. There may be a lengthy waiting list for another treatment center. It also may take the person a while to look for treatment again. There are many reasons being turned away from treatment can be damaging. In my view, there are already enough reasons people are turned away that are entirely out of the control of the individual or even the center, e.g., the cost of treatment and related insurance coverage. Unlike many other reasons for which a person might not have access to treatment, veganism is one that can possibly be avoided.

Looking for treatment can be an exhausting prospect. Eating disorders have a substantially negative impact on quality of life (van Hoeken &

Hoek, 2020). According to Carrie Hunnicutt (n.d.), senior vice president of business development for Monte Nido & Affiliates,

> Across all eating disorder conditions, disordered thoughts and actions can quickly lead to compulsions that threaten to overtake every minute of daily life. Without care at effective eating disorder treatment centers, patients often work overtime attempting to maintain habits centered around eating disorder symptoms.

The longer a person goes without treatment, the greater the likelihood of eating disorder–related debilitation. Indeed, Hunnicutt says, "Any delay in acquiring treatment for eating disorders can lead to physical and mental health complications for the patient."

It is therefore reasonable to presume that by the time a vegan patient has gotten themselves through the door of a non-vegan treatment center, they are likely at the point of being severely compromised by their sickness. I believe this is because the reasons for not permitting veganism in treatment are largely uninvestigated in the eating disorder community. Since Brown et al. (2019) specified that non-negotiables must be thoroughly investigated, I believe the community could do more to reliably assess the supposed necessity and subsequent generalization of this treatment non-negotiable. I believe if we can thoroughly assess veganism's non-negotiable status in advance of applying it, then we can prevent it from being applied across the board and in black-and-white terms.

It must be said that accepting vegan clients into an eating disorder treatment program does not equate to denying that they may be using veganism to cover an eating disorder. Highlighting this, the Recover Clinic—a mental health clinic founded by Emmy Brunner, MSC, PGDIP, BA HONS—works with vegan patients; even so, Brunner acknowledges that the label of veganism could serve as a socially acceptable form of restriction. Additionally, Beasley acknowledges that "some eating disorder clients misuse veganism as a means to control or as a cover for restricting food choices" (Beasley, 2020). However, both the Recover Clinic and Alsana ensure that a patient's veganism does not serve as a barrier to barrier to receiving treatment.

Veganism (Non-Negotiable) and Vegetarianism (Negotiable?): Is There a Line?

Many people believe that treating a vegetarian patient but not a vegan patient is possible. Therefore, a fair number of treatment centers allow vegetarianism but draw the line at veganism. I am curious as to why there is an assured allowance for vegetarianism, especially because vegetarians, too, worry about the presence of animals in their food (e.g., mistakenly being served chicken broth) and follow rules (e.g., not eating animals). These qualifiers, while not identical, are similar in veganism, and yet a cut-off point has been defined. I believe this distinction highlights the arbitrarily subjective nature of determining what is best for a particular patient.

It is true that recovery from eating disorders often entails lessening rigidity and all-or-nothing thinking in eating and other aspects of life. I personally felt unworthy while experiencing my eating disorder; it is no wonder I subjected myself to mental anguish upon having an extra bite of a particular snack. However, in truth, there is no hard-and-fast rule regarding vegetarianism versus veganism; no marked line that determines whether recovery is possible on one side and impossible on the other.

Furthermore, black-or-white mentalities can counter the very essence of recovery. My own experience with an eating disorder involved perceiving both my inner and outer worlds as black or white. The eating disorder benefits from a lack of nuance; recovery, on the other hand, recognizes nuance. Veganism ought to only be considered a non-negotiable once an eating disordered person has been assessed for treatment; determining whether there should be any negotiation regarding following a vegan food plan should be part of the treatment process. It is up to the discretion of the treatment provider to determine when and how a vegan food plan should be implemented. The treatment provider may well conclude that a non-vegan food plan should be implemented immediately upon the person entering treatment. But this assessment cannot be rightly made before the treatment process has officially started.

As we can see, many beliefs about veganism in relation to eating disorders influence professional perspectives and plans for treatment. Veganism, in my opinion, is often prematurely regarded as a form of eating disordered restriction. Ensuring that vegan patients are given the best possible chance at a full recovery necessitates forming a foundational belief that they can fully recover under optimal conditions. One of these conditions is that professionals thoroughly examine any assumptive "if this, then that" logic when it comes to eating disordered vegan individuals. How did we arrive at this logic? How can we make it less black and white? Ultimately, how can we do our best by each patient in accordance with what will help them?

References

Barnett, M. J., Dripps, W. R., & Blomquist, K. K. (2016). Organivore or organorexic? Examining the relationship between alternative food network engagement, disordered eating, and special diets. *Appetite, 105*, 713–720. https://doi.org/10.1016/j.appet.2016.07.008

Beasley, T. (R. D. N.) (2020, May 15). Veganism and eating disorder recovery. Alsana®. Retrieved April 3, 2022, from www.alsana.com/blog/eating-disorder-recovery-bringing-vegans-into-the-fold/

Briones, J. (2019, January 9). My story: How I used veganism to heal my eating disorder. *Sweet Simple Vegan*. Retrieved August 15, 2022, from https://sweetsimplevegan.com/2015/02/mystory/

Brown, A., Fuller, S., & Simic, M. (2019). *Consensus statement on considerations for treating vegan patients with eating disorders The Royal College of Psychiatrists, The British Dietetic Association and BEAT.* www.rcpsych.ac.uk/docs/default-source/members/faculties/eating-disorders/vegan-patients-eating-disorders-mar19.pdf?sfvrsn=be96d428_2

Brytek-Matera, A., Czepczor-Bernat, K., Jurzak, H., Kornacka, M., & Kołodziejczyk, N. (2018). Strict health-oriented eating patterns (orthorexic eating behaviours) and their connection with a vegetarian and vegan diet. *Eating and Weight Disorders: EWD, 24*(3), 441–452. https://doi.org/10.1007/s40519-018-0563-5

Geller, J., Goodrich, S., Chan, K., Cockell, S., & Srikameswaran, S. (2012, September 1). Clinical practice guidelines for the British Columbia eating disorder continuum of services. *InsideOut*. https://insideoutinstitute.org.au/resource-library/clinical-practice-guidelines-for-the-british-columbia-eating-disorder-continuum-of-services

Goodman, D., & Goodman, M. K. (2007). *Localism, livelihoods and the 'post-organic': Changing perspectives on alternative food networks in the United States.* Elsevier.

Hunnicutt, C. (n.d.). Impact of eating disorders on quality of life—and how treatment centers can help. *Monte Nido*. Retrieved April 3, 2022, from www.montenido.com/impact-of-eating-disorders/

Kofsky, R. (2020, July 27). *Veganism and eating disorders. Integrated eating* (M. S. Mora, Ed.). www.integratedeating.com/blog/2020/7/27/veganism-and-eating-disorders.

Mann, C. (2018). *Vystopia: The anguish of being vegan in a non-vegan world.* Communicate31 Pty Ltd.

van Hoeken, D., & Hoek, H. W. (2020). Review of the burden of eating disorders: Mortality, disability, costs, quality of life, and family burden. *Current Opinion in Psychiatry, 33*(6), 521–527. https://doi.org/10.1097/YCO.0000000000000641

5

THE IMPORTANCE OF UNDERSTANDING MOTIVATION FOR VEGANISM

Vegans are ethically motivated to adopt a vegan lifestyle. Food is only one aspect of this lifestyle, so it is fair to say that vegans with eating disorders still have their ethical beliefs. Identifying whether an eating disordered client follows an ethical vegan belief system is crucial for implementing effective treatment. This treatment extends to after-care planning, including setting up vegan-specific supportive resources as needed. This continued support might reasonably extend to food options, social networks, and less intensive treatment programs that accommodate vegans.

Although veganism may be a disguise for an underlying eating disorder, alternative explanations can also be true. Thus, I advocate for determining motivation for a dietary choice on an individualized basis. As discussed, the data show efficacy in accounting for motivation. This data includes research articles whose findings suggest that ethical vegans and ethical vegetarians may be less inclined to have an eating disorder than individuals who are drawn toward veganism and vegetarianism for health and/or dietary

DOI: 10.4324/9781003310617-7

reasons. It is therefore important that we assess not only motivation itself but the rationale behind it.

Encouraging a patient to understand their own motivation is treatment-progressive. After all, the patient is in treatment not only to recover from their eating disorder but also to better understand themselves. If an eating disorder professional presumes that veganism compromises recovery, the importance of establishing an eating disordered individual's vegan motivation might be unfairly undermined. Indeed, to doubt a patient's ability to know themselves is to doubt their ability to recover.

Questioning a Patient's Reality

Professionals understand that it is generally not a good idea to challenge a patient's core self. There is no therapeutic benefit to questioning a patient's authentic reality. However, the eating disordered person is typically internally conflicted. Their real self is in there somewhere, but the eating disordered voice is likely not going anywhere without a fight.

Problems can subsequently arise when professionals assume they are addressing the sick part of an eating disordered person's mind when they are actually addressing the person's authentic self. Certainly, questioning the eating disorder's reality is fair game in treatment. However, questioning the reality of *anything* that does not relate to the eating disorder is risky at best and potentially damaging at worst. Indeed, in her (2020) Alsana blog post, Tammy Beasley, MS, RDN, CEDS-S, LD, says, "Eating disorders carry lots of food beliefs, but having strong food beliefs does not always mean you have an eating disorder" (Alsana, 2020). This line of thinking contributed to Alsana's acceptance of vegans into its treatment programs. In a similar vein, Senior Nutrition Leadership at Accanto Health, the parent company of The Emily Program and Veritas Collaborative, says that its program take vegetarian and vegan preferences "at face value" and "work with vegetarians and vegans at all levels of care" (Accanto Health, personal communication, March 16, 2022).

The distinction between what is and is not coming from the eating disorder must be carefully gauged. Only once this distinction has been made can veganism be addressed through a recovery-oriented lens. Regarding her approach with clients, Beasley (2020) says,

> I do not want to doubt the sincerity of my vegan clients based on assumptions or suspicions. I believe it is my job and the job of my team to help each individual, regardless of their feeding preference, get honest about what's behind those preferences and see if we can untangle the ethical vegan beliefs from the eating disorder.

Similarly, Integrated Eating's staff dietician Rachel Kofsky (2020) says,

> The challenge in treatment is helping our vegan clients decipher if this dietary choice is influenced by their eating disorder. We consider if their choice to limit animal-based foods is driven by the eating disorder or true personal wants. This is what recovery is all about!

We must try our best to identify the part of the patient that is true to them and the part of the patient that has been hijacked by the eating disorder.

Because identifying ethical motivation can inform a patient's treatment trajectory, it is vital that the eating disorder field notes the findings in the following research studies: In her 2014 master's thesis, "Comparing vegan and vegetarian attitudes, beliefs and perceptions with risk for disordered eating behaviors," Chaya Lee Charles (2014) grouped vegetarians and vegans together in some of her findings, but still recognized that "those with weight motivation for dietary choices were found to be at a heightened risk for disordered eating", indicating the significance of motivation. Charles also saw "higher disordered eating behavior in vegetarians (especially lacto-ovo vegetarians) than vegans," concluding that, since "health/weight motivated vegetarians appeared to be at higher risk for disordered eating than the rest of the group," then "evaluation of dietary motivation is crucial in establishing potential risk for disordered eating." Highlighting the importance of consistently applied accurate definitions in interpreting research outcomes, Charles says, those who "do not truly follow a vegetarian or vegan diet (when compared to operationalized definitions) have a higher risk of disordered behaviors than true vegans/vegetarians." (Charles, 2014, pp. 1–2).

On the surface, Brytek-Matera et al. might seem to suggest that vegans are more likely to have orthorexia nervosa (ON) by stating that

"the prevalence of ON in the vegan (7.9%) and vegetarian groups (3.8%) are higher than in the individuals consuming meat (3.6% of participants with rare meat consumption and 0% of participants with frequent meat consumption)" (2018, p. 449).

However, upon a closer look, since health-based vegans and ethically-based vegans are included in the same category in this study, we can see that definitions were initially conflated. As discussed in this book's introduction, health-based vegans are akin to plant-based eaters, whereas veganism is ethically based. It follows that the results of Brytek-Matera et al.'s study establish a link between health motivation and orthorexia, but no link, no link between ethical motivation and orthorexia. This finding leads to Brytek-Matera et al.'s conclusion that "ethical causes might be a protective factor in the development of eating behaviours as a cognitive aspect in this group."

Brytek-Matera et al. (2018) also acknowledge two relevant limitations: (1) "We evaluated a posteriori the reason for following a meat-free diet, and the number of individuals choosing ethical versus health reasons was not equivalent" and (2) "we did not assess emotional distress related to food choices" (p. 450). The first limitation matters because, as other studies echo, ethical reasoning is a factor in determining the link between veganism and eating disorders. The second limitation matters because emotional distress around food choices is a marker of an eating disordered mentality. Its inclusion in this study may have influenced the conditions under which orthorexia was assessed. This avoidable conflation has played its role in shaping the prevailing eating disorder field narrative. Let us also consider Brytek-Matera et al.'s assertion that "following diet and lifestyle recommendations for a well-balanced vegetarian diet could be helpful for individuals with eating behaviours to better plan both the quality and quantity of their meals" (p. 450). It seems that they acknowledge that their findings do not negate the possibility that vegetarianism and orthorexia recovery can co-exist.

In the interest of accuracy, let us look at the research of Barthels et al. (2018), to which Brytek-Matera et al. (2018) refer. The latter references the former in support of its findings being "in line with the results of the latest research, which have shown that vegetarians and vegans do not differ in orthorexic eating behaviour, but both groups presented higher level of orthorexic eating behaviour than individuals with rare and frequent meat consumption" (p. 449). Barthels et al. (2018) acknowledge higher—albeit non-pathological—levels of "orthorexic eating behaviour" among "vegans and vegetarians . . . than individuals who consume red meat" (p. 164); they also acknowledge that "prevalence rates for orthorexia in the vegan and vegetarian group are higher than in the groups not restricting their eating behaviour" (p. 164), thereby suggesting "that restricting one's eating behaviour regarding food of animal origin might serve as a risk factor for developing orthorexic eating behaviour" (p. 164). However, omitted from the Brytek-Matera et al. article is Barthels et al.'s mention of a motivational signifier, as "unpublished data from [their] workgroup suggest that in vegans, only health-related motives are associated with orthorexic eating behaviour, whereas ethical reasons are not, indicating that underlying motives and beliefs might moderate this effect" (Barthels et al., 2018, p. 164).

Barthels et al. (2019) accurately state that orthorexia is linked to health rather than animal welfare. However, they inaccurately go on to group concerns for personal health and animal welfare under veganism. Their study "concluded that underlying motives and not observable eating behavior form risk factors for developing an orthorexic eating behavior" (p. 819). Additionally, the authors found "that orthorexic eating behavior is associated with the importance of the underlying motives health, esthetics and healing, whereas animal welfare, politics and ecology are not linked to orthorexia" (p. 817), such that "this study reveals that a vegan lifestyle is not per se associated with eating behavior, but rather that it varies with the underlying motivation for following a vegan diet."

A study by Norwood et al. misleadingly grouped together "vegetarian, vegan, gluten free, paleo and weight loss" clients when measuring their data against that of "a comparison group who were not following a specific dietary pattern." While the formation of the initial group might merge categories that do not belong together, it is worth acknowledging the study's separate "health-motivation" category. The researchers' distinction of this category allowed the following finding to come to light:

> The weight loss diet group tended to be the most extreme in its psychological characteristics, showing poorer psychological wellbeing and less healthy eating attitudes and behaviours, as well as lower self-control and self-efficacy. By contrast, the vegetarian, vegan and especially the paleo groups showed characteristics of relative psychological strength, including more helpful and health-motivated eating behaviours.
>
> (Norwood et al., 2019, p. 148)

Additionally, the researchers found that

> the psychological characteristics of the weight loss group showed the greatest number of extreme and negative values compared with the other dietary groups. Generally, the weight loss group reported significantly lower psychological well-being and a greater presence of unhelpful eating attitudes and behaviours.
>
> (p. 155)

A 2018 study by Çiçekoğlu and Tunçay, conducted in Turkey, grouped vegans and vegetarians together in their study. However, their results warrant consideration. While their study found "that [vegans/vegetarians] had a higher risk of eating disorders than the nonvegans/nonvegetarians" (p. 204), it also found that "non-vegans/vegetarians had more obsessive symptoms and were more orthorectic than the vegans/vegetarians" (p. 203), that there was "not a significant difference in attitudes to eating, obsessive symptoms and orthorexia scores between the vegans/vegetarians and the nonvegans/nonvegetarians," and that orthorexia nervosa "scores and obsessive symptoms did not significantly differ between the vegans/vegetarians and the nonvegans/nonvegetarians in terms of gender, marital status, age, BMI, education and doing exercise" (p. 203). For the purposes of assessing motivation in patients, it is worth mentioning Çiçekoğlu and Tunçay's finding that "individuals becoming a vegan/vegetarian for ethical reasons consume more desserts and fat than those becoming a vegan/ vegetarian for health reasons" (p. 204). The authors ultimately concluded "that the vegans/vegetarians' attitudes towards eating did not have a risk of orthorexia and that they adopted veganism/vegetarianism for ethical reasons, not for good health" (p. 204).

Curtis and Comer's (2006) study about feminism, eating disorders, and body image found that "semi-vegetarians who cited weight as one of the top three reasons behind their eating style reported significantly higher levels of dietary restraint than did non-weight-motivated semi-vegetarians and both weight-motivated and non-weight-motivated full vegetarians." As such, the authors recommend that "semi- and full vegetarians are fundamentally different and therefore should be examined separately in terms of dietary restraint and related phenomena" (Curtis & Comer, 2006, pp. 99–101).

Timko et al. (2012) help to clarify that which Curtis and Comer (2006) left open-ended by breaking down broader categories into "vegans," "vegetarians," "semi-vegetarians," and "non-vegetarians," thus allowing for greater accuracy. With that, they ultimately found "semi-vegetarians, but not full vegetarians or vegans, are most likely to engage in disordered eating behaviors," (p. 987) and similarly "that semi-vegetarians had the most pathological relationship with food and the body" (p. 988).

Heiss et al. (2017), in their literature review, show support for the specification of categories in the interest of accurate research outcomes. They concluded from their research that:

> vegans and vegetarians typically endorse significantly lower levels of restraint and external eating, and greater levels of food acceptance, in comparison to semi-vegetarians. These findings suggest that semi-vegetarians are categorically different from ovolactovegetarians and vegans, and this distinction should be considered when assessing diet type and pathological eating.
>
> (Heiss et al., 2017, p. 67)

In a later study, Heiss et al. (2018) found that "more research is needed to determine the suitability of the EDE-Q for quantifying eating behaviors, including in those abstaining from animal products" (p. 418). Heiss et al. found that:

in clinical samples, not only is the type of vegetarianism important to assess but also the reason and timing of vegetarian diet. The latter is particularly important in determining whether vegetarianism played a causal role in the development of the eating disorder.

(p. 67)

Likewise, Heiss et al. acknowledged a need for further methodological specificity, stating that

across studies comparing subgroups of vegetarians, consistent trends have emerged that indicate a definitive need for distinguishing between different types of meat avoiders. . . . When compared to true vegetarians, vegans, and omnivores, it appears the semivegetarians are the "most pathological."

(2017, p. 66)

The issue of timing is also important when assessing a person's commitment to ethical veganism. Paslakis et al. only required a minimum two-week veganism and vegetarianism commitment to qualify for their study. This is notably contrary to a study conducted by McDonald (2000) on the process of becoming vegan, which required participants to have been vegan for at least one year. As such, Paslakis et al.'s study hardly accounts for a genuine appraisal of either veganism or vegetarianism; yet it concludes that "higher eating disorder-related psychopathology" was "significantly associated with vegetarian/vegan diets" (Paslakis et al., 2020).

Timko et al. found that "vegans and true vegetarians had significantly lower levels of restraint, external eating, hedonic hunger, and greater levels of acceptance in relation to food in comparison to semi-vegetarians" and that, in fact, "vegans appear to have the healthiest attitudes towards food, closely followed by vegetarians. Non-vegetarians more closely resemble semi-vegetarians, though as noted the former have more maladaptive attitudes" (2012, p. 989).

According to Bardone-Cone et al. (2012, p. 1250), "From an eating disorders perspective, individuals who are sincerely motivated to adopt vegetarianism for primarily nonweight reasons (eg, ethics)

may be less concerning than individuals with weight-based motives."
Additionally, Hamilton's finding that "aversion to meat tends to be
most clearly associated with an ethical stance against the consumption
of meat rather than with health concerns" might indicate the importance of determining vegan motivation (2006, p. 157). If meat aversion
is more closely linked to ethics than it is to health, then identifying
such aversion in an eating disordered patient could help to clarify
whether the root of their deterrence is rational or irrational. Although
Bardone-Cone et al.'s and Hamilton's research included vegetarians
and not vegans, I will speculate that their statements might, by extension, apply to vegans.

Orthorexia and Ethics

As seen, a variety of research findings indicate that health-motivated
vegans are more likely to restrict food than ethically motivated
vegans. We should consider these findings when discussing orthorexia nervosa, which is "an obsession with proper or 'healthful'
eating" (National Eating Disorders Association). Since orthorexia is
associated with irrational aims toward health, it is possible that certain individuals who say they became vegan due to a health motivation might have instead become vegan due to a health obsession
(which, of course, connotes the very opposite of a rational health
motivation).

It is possible that an ethically vegan person and an orthorexic person
may each refuse to eat the same piece of animal food, but, the orthorexic
person's refusal would be based on an obsession with health, whereas the
vegan person's refusal would be based on ethics.

This health-versus-ethics distinction should also apply to a person who
is both orthorexic and vegan. So, if presented with the option to consume
the least processed part of an animal (possessing a level of "healthful-
ness" that might satisfy an orthorexic mindset), the vegan part of them
would probably refrain. However, the orthorexic vegan may refuse to eat
vegan food on health grounds. So, if presented with the option to consume vegan food that they considered unhealthy, the orthorexic part of

them would likely resist. Indeed, Registered Dietitian and ethical vegan Gena Hamshaw says,

> The primary distinction is that I choose not to eat animals for ethical reasons, and not because I think that they're 'bad' for me, or because I think they'll make me gain weight. Put differently, veganism feels like a moral imperative to me at this point.
>
> (Hamshaw, 2016)

In Sum

Identifying motivation is important to vegans for many reasons. First, it can allow the treatment team to better understand the patient. If professionals can better understand their patient, they can better work with them. Second, it can help in contributing to decisions made about vegan dietary allowance. Third, it can help in providing the necessary and, if needed, vegan-specific support this person might need with any non-vegan elements of their treatment.

As a field, we should acknowledge research saying that ethically motivated vegans have higher recovery outcomes. We might consider the extent to which their veganism is motivated by the part of them that wants to recover. Because veganism, unlike the eating disorder, can feel like an authentic part of a person's identity, perhaps it can serve as a powerful recovery motivator.

Vegans find a sense of purpose in living according to their vegan ethics. Therefore, so long as treatment is effective in determining that they are acting of their volition rather than that of their eating disorder; so long as treatment determines that eating vegan is physically, psychologically, and pragmatically possible for them; and so long as veganism really is what they want, then I reason that the dietary component of veganism should be regarded as vital to their continued recovery and thus—bearing in mind the "possible and practicable" component of veganism—permitted to the fullest extent.

References

Bardone-Cone, A. M., Fitzsimmons-Craft, E. E., Harney, M. B., Maldonado, C. R., Lawson, M. A., Smith, R., & Robinson, D. P. (2012). The inter-relationships between vegetarianism and eating disorders among females. *Journal of the Academy of Nutrition and Dietetics, 112*(8), 1247–1252. https://doi.org/10.1016/j.jand.2012.05.007

Barthels, F., Meyer, F., & Pietrowsky, R. (2018). and restrained eating behaviour in vegans, vegetarians, and individuals on a diet. *Eat and Weight Disorders, 23*, 159–166 https://doi.org/10.1007/s40519-018-0479-0

Barthels, F., Poerschke, S., Müller, R., & Pietrowsky, R. (2019). eating behavior in vegans is linked to health, not to animal welfare. *Eat and Weight Disorders, 25*(3), 817–820. https://doi.org/10.1007/s40519-019-00679-8

Beasley, T. (R. D. N.) (2020, May 15). *Veganism and eating disorder recovery.* Alsana®. Retrieved April 3, 2022, from www.alsana.com/blog/eating-disorder-recovery-bringing-vegans-into-the-fold/

Brytek-Matera, A., Czepczor-Bernat, K., Jurzak, H., Kornacka, M., & Kołodziejczyk, N. (2018). Strict health-oriented eating patterns (ortho-rexic eating behaviours) and their connection with a vegetarian and vegan diet. *Eating and Weight Disorders: EWD, 24*(3), 441–452. https://doi.org/10.1007/s40519-018-0563-5

Charles, C. L. (2014) *Comparing vegan and vegetarian attitudes, beliefs and perceptions with risk for disordered eating behaviors* (1572484) [Dissertation, Syracuse University]. ProQuest Dissertations Publishing. https://search.proquest.com/docview/1651204516/?pq-origsite=primo

Çiçekoğlu, P., & Tunçay, G. Y. (2018). A comparison of eating attitudes between vegans/vegetarians and nonvegans/nonvegetarians in terms of orthorexia nervosa. *Archives of Psychiatric Nursing, 32*(2), 200–205. www.psychiatricnursing.org/article/S0883-9417(17)30154-1/fulltext

Curtis, M. J., & Comer, L. K. (2006). Vegetarianism, dietary restraint and feminist identity. *Eating Behaviors, 7*(2), 91–104. https://doi.org/10.1016/j.eatbeh.2005.08.002

Hamilton, M. (2006). Disgust reactions to meat among ethically and health motivated vegetarians. *Ecology of Food and Nutrition, 45*(2), 125–158. https://doi.org/10.1080/03670240500530691

Hamshaw, G. (2016, November 23). On veganism, eating disorder recovery, and "No" foods. *The Full Helping*. Retrieved April 6, 2022, from www.thefullhelping.com/on-veganism-eating-disorder-recovery-and-no-foods/

Heiss, S., Boswell, J. F., & Hormes, J. M. (2018). Confirmatory factor analysis of the eating disorder examination-questionnaire: A comparison of five factor solutions across vegan and omnivore participants. *International Journal of Eating Disorders, 51*(5), 418–428. https://doi.org/10.1002/eat.22848

Heiss, S., Hormes, J. M., & Alix Timko, C. (2017). Vegetarianism and eating disorders. *Vegetarian and Plant-Based Diets in Health and Disease Prevention*, 51–69. https://doi.org/10.1016/b978-0-12-803968-7.00004-6

Kofsky, R. (2020, July 27). Veganism and eating disorders. In M. S. Mora (Ed.), *Integrated eating*. www.integratedeating.com/blog/2020/7/27/veganism-and-eating-disorders.

McDonald, B. (2000). "Once you know something, you can't not know it": An empirical look at becoming vegan. *Society & Animals, 8*(1), 1–23. https://doi.org/10.1163/156853000x00011

Norwood, R., Cruwys, T., Chachay, V. S., & Sheffield, J. (2019). The psychological characteristics of people consuming vegetarian, vegan, paleo, gluten free and weight loss dietary patterns. *Obesity Science & Practice, 5*(2), 148–158. https://doi.org/10.1002/osp4.325

Paslakis, G., Richardson, C., Nöhre, M., Brähler, E., Holzapfel, C., Hilbert, A., & de Zwaan, M. (2020). Prevalence and psychopathology of vegetarians and vegans – Results from a 167 representative survey in Germany. *Scientific Reports, 10*(1). https://doi.org/10.1038/s41598-020-63910-y

Timko, C. A., Hormes, J. M., & Chubski, J. (2012). Will the real vegetarian please stand up? An investigation of dietary restraint and eating disorder symptoms in vegetarians versus non-vegetarians. *Appetite, 58*(3), 982–990. https://doi.org/10.1016/j.appet.2012.02.005

Section II

VEGAN EXPERIENCES

In Section I, we found our footing. In Section II, we dig deeper. Section I said, "This is going on. This is how it happened and now here we are." It pointed us out on a map. Now that we know where we are, we may thoroughly assess the terrain.

A lot of people don't want to talk about what I present in Section II. But we have reached a critical threshold that necessitates talking. So now that we have found our footing, let us familiarize ourselves with differences between eating disorders and veganism. This will lead us to a discussion of the vegan experience, which will culminate in an exploration of how that experience might affect a vegan patient who is receiving non-vegan treatment. How might the vegan person feel and why? This section takes a deeper dive into the need for vegan-specific professional understanding and support.

DOI: 10.4324/9781003310617-8

6

CONFLATING CONCEPTS: PERFECTIONISM, MORALITY, FREEDOM

We have established that veganism and eating disorders are two separate concepts, not to be assumptively conflated with one another. While previous chapters have focused primarily on the differences between eating disordered restriction and the dietary component of veganism, this chapter will distinguish in greater depth the pathological versus non-pathological nature of eating disorders as a whole versus veganism as a whole. Knowing the differences will allow eating disorder professionals to consider this topic as fairly as possible.

Perfectionism

Let us begin by focusing on the concept of perfectionism. There are key differences between veganism and eating disorders when it comes to the idea of perfectionism. Since a vegan strives to do the best they

DOI: 10.4324/9781003310617-9

can for animals, the vegan's perfectionism is therefore directed toward animals rather than toward themselves. However, perfectionism as it relates to eating disorders is directed toward the self. Furthermore, an understanding of imperfection is embedded in the essence of veganism. We live in a primarily non-vegan world, and therefore, vegans cannot be expected to live a life in perfect accordance with vegan ethics. In "(seeking) to exclude—as far as is possible and practicable—all forms of exploitation of, and cruelty to, animals for food, clothing or any other purpose" (The Vegan Society), the words, "as far as is possible and practicable" encompass this inability to attain perfection. Indeed, the acceptance of imperfection is built into the vegan philosophy. It is not possible to lead a perfectly vegan life, but vegans consciously do everything in their power to live according to vegan values.

The opposite of eating disordered perfectionism is freedom; the opposite of vegan perfectionism is understanding that while imperfection is the reality, the ideal is unattainable in a non-vegan world. Ideally, animals would never have to be harmed for our use. Hence, falling short of perfectionism in veganism serves as an indicator of societal reliance on animal products. An eating disordered person might regard the loosening of their rigid, self-imposed food rules as imperfection; however, eating disorder treatment providers might regard this sign of imperfection as an aspect of recovery.

Veganism equates striving toward perfection with progress—wholly opposite to eating disorders, which equates embracing a perceived imperfection with progress. Vegans' acceptance that they cannot be perfectly ethical is not considered a reason to incorporate non-vegan food into their diets. Rather, vegans interpret this imperfection as the cue to keep doing what they are doing—not do *less* of it. The goal of a vegan is not to be perfect; rather, it is to do the best one can, considering the pervasiveness of animal exploitation. Therefore, tendencies toward vegan-related perfectionism can be addressed through *education* because education *informs* rather than *treats*. By contrast, eating-disorder related perfectionism can be addressed through *treatment* because treatment aims to challenge the perfectionistic component of eating disorders.

Ethically based vegans are capable of recognizing that they have a wide variety of food to eat; therefore, a recovery goal for an ethical vegan would be an ability to eat all kinds of vegan food where none of it is off-limits. Vegans in eating disorder recovery are not saying they are going to live on a sterile planet somewhere in the distant galaxy in a hazmat suit to avoid even the slightest touch of a non-vegan trace ingredient that they might accidentally breathe in from someone eating a non-vegan crumb cake five rooms away. Vegans are aware of the realities of the world they are living in, and treatment providers should understand their vegan patients' best intentions. A vegan's intention may be to enjoy a rich nutritional varied diet including desserts without being governed by the eating disorder's rules. Both vegans and non-vegans understand that their recovery entails the practice of flexibility and adaptivity as they go along. According to Taylor Wolfram, MS, RDN, LDN, the term "as far as is possible and practicable . . . brings flexibility and inclusivity to veganism. It acknowledges that the world in which we live is heavily reliant on animals and that it's not realistic to avoid every single form of animal exploitation" (Wolfram, 2019).

Importantly, if someone with an eating disorder who is vegan chooses a recovery path that involves incorporating a part—but not all—of their veganism, this is done for the benefit of their eating disorder recovery. However, it is important to note that incorporating a part of veganism is not an automatic option for vegans. Therefore, a vegan person in recovery would not necessarily be comfortable taking away some—but not all—of their veganism. Just as the pursuit of recovery would entail leaving all and not just most of the eating disorder behind, so would the pursuit of veganism entail incorporation of as much of it into life as possible. The vegan person who is voluntarily forgoing part of the dietary component of veganism for the sake of their recovery is, in fact, doing as much as is "possible and practicable." Additionally, some vegans may consider maintenance of veganism's dietary component necessary for their recovery. In this way, if it has been deemed benefi-cial for a patient to remain vegan after treatment, they can still adhere to their own personal standard in accordance with their individualized treatment plan.

Morality: "Good/Safe Foods" Versus "Bad/Feared Foods"

Often, people with eating disorders distinguish between what their eating disordered mindset deems "good" versus "bad" food. They perceive good food as food that their eating disordered mindset would deem acceptable and in keeping with its set of (unattainable) standards. They perceive bad food as impermissible, its consumption warranting negative self-talk. The basis of this good-versus-bad determination, while justifiable to the eating disordered mind, is arbitrary—pertaining only to the experience of a particular person and subject to vast differentiation from one eating disordered person to the next. Similarly, people with eating disorders frequently have "fear foods," juxtaposed with eating disorder–approved "safe foods." Fear foods are resisted by the eating disordered person to assuage the eating disordered mindset. Foods that are deemed "bad" are often synonymously considered "scary," while foods that are deemed "good" are often synonymously considered "safe."

Assigning morality to food is counterintuitive to recovery. It is therefore important to delve into what makes something "good" versus "bad" according to the eating disorder's mindset alongside what makes something "good" versus "bad" according to a vegan mindset. Eating disordered perceptions of "good" and "bad" food often imply personal goodness or badness. This relationship between the dichotomy of good/ bad food and good/bad person should be challenged in treatment. Since eating disorders can be heavily wrapped up in identity (Stanghellini et al., 2012; Stein & Corte, 2006), and identity can consist of moral stances, it is wise to dissuade eating disordered individuals from assigning such value to food.

When an eating disordered person uses the words "good" and "bad" to describe food, we assume there is an implied self-judgment. However, this implication does not automatically apply to a vegan person who uses these words about non-vegan food. This is because rejection of the notion that animals are food does not indicate an inability to view food in neutral terms. Vegans regard eating meat as unconscionable because they register it as part of a formerly sentient animal. They cannot seamlessly separate the animal-derived item on their plate from that animal's former sentience. Their visceral reaction might be what Hamilton (2006, p. 157) referred to as both "revulsion" and "disgust." However, the revulsion and disgust are primarily directed toward the food rather than toward the self, at least on a surface level. The root of the problem is essentially external, to which internal feelings would be an effect. Hamilton (2006, p. 157) explains this position by saying there exists:

> a genuinely ethical stance that leads some to avoid meat consumption . . . as a consequence of this ethical stance entailing an identification between humans and animals, involves feelings of disgust, revulsion, and horror in the face of the products of violence and taking of life much like those felt in the face of taking human life and dismemberment of human bodies.

By contrast, an eating disorder often involves disgust with oneself. The disgust is negative, something to be worked through and ultimately released. Veganism involves disgust with animal exploitation. It is not a vegan's ultimate goal to stop being disgusted; rather, a vegan's feeling of disgust can be considered contextually appropriate. A vegan would use this disgust consciously to propel them toward positive change.

Vegan disgust is rational; eating disordered disgust is irrational. For the vegan, the feelings around eating a piece of fried chicken are not the same as the feelings around eating a piece of fried seitan. For me, the feelings around eating the latter would have been solely related to my eating disorder. The disgust, terror, worry, dread, and self-loathing would have been about my eating disorder. While the act of eating in and of itself would have been related to my eating disorder, the feelings about eating the piece of chicken in particular would have been about eating someone else. My aversion to the chicken that I mentioned in Chapter 1 was not about an aversion to food; it was about an aversion to eating an animal. It would be the same aversion I would have had if someone had put a cooked dog in front of me. My vegan disgust did not originate from my eating disorder but rather from myself.

When considering "fear foods," it is important to account for the ethical components of a patient's dietary choices. What is "fear" in a vegan context? Furthermore, what is "food"? Can types of food that one's ethics disqualify as consumable count as fear food? Or are there entirely different qualifiers for why a vegan would feel aversive to certain foods? Let us consider that vegans see animal-based food on their plate not as something but rather as someone. Let us further consider that, for vegans, the idea of eating "someone" is unfathomable, regardless of particularities. For example, a vegan person would not consider chicken a "fear food" while simultaneously considering lamb a "safe food." So while eating disordered fear foods may seem arbitrary to a non-eating-disordered person, a vegan's omitted foods are objectively classifiable. An eating disordered person challenging themselves to eat their fear foods is not to be conflated with a vegan person challenging themselves to eat animals and animal by-products. The eating disordered mindset may express itself as having a fear of a particular food, but this fear is often rooted in an avoidance of experiencing emotional pain that the person may not feel equipped to experience (Henderson et al., 2019; Costin, 2007; Costin & Grabb, 2012). A vegan person has an *aversion* to eating animals rather than a *fear*.

In treatment, a vegan eating disordered person can learn that there is no such thing as "good" versus "bad" food in exactly the same way a non-vegan eating disordered person can. Abandoning the "good versus bad food" mentality is a sign of recovery—whether vegan or not. The choices available to a vegan may be different to a degree, but a vegan's progress ought to be measured alongside that of their non-vegan counterpart. (See Chapter 12 for professional assessment considerations.)

Freedom

Recovering from an eating disorder means attaining freedom from eating disordered behaviors, urges, and thoughts. Sufferers can attain this freedom by eating their "fear foods" with consistent, supported practice. The goal is that the person will eventually disassociate the food from their fear and, instead, feel neutral toward the food. This is when it becomes especially important to remember that a vegan's avoidance of non-vegan food does not equate to a compromised sense of freedom. To the contrary, the vegan would feel less free by being made to eat non-vegan food because they are eating something out of alignment with their values. Eating animals, to a vegan, is a non-option. Vegans find freedom in refraining from animal food.

I acknowledge that treatment centers may recognize that when patients leave treatment, the world to which they are returning is one in which their veganism will not be the societal standard. They may regard non-vegan eating in recovery as an understandable necessity toward preparing for daily life as a recovering person in a primarily non-vegan world. Treatment, in the hope of giving a vegan patient an optimal chance of sustained recovery, might aim to resemble the dietary components of a primarily non-vegan world as closely as possible.

However, as mentioned in the discussion of perfectionism, vegans, too, recognize that the world is not vegan, which is precisely why their veganism should be carefully considered. Recovery should entail learning how to navigate the world in a way that best benefits their recovery. How is a vegan patient supposed to prepare for eating vegan once they're recovered if their recovery process consisted of non-vegan food? How does neglecting to prepare people to eat in accordance with their values help them?

Indeed, so long as anyone is eating with a recovery mindset, thriving in recovery is possible. Why not offer the vegan person the chance to practice with that mindset during treatment alongside non-vegans? A major part of recovery is repeatedly choosing what is right for oneself, even when the world says otherwise. Therefore, just as treatment would prepare a person to trust their treatment plan amidst the flurry of diet-fad information, so too would adequate treatment prepare a vegan to stay true to their own needs in a world that does not fundamentally cater to vegans. In an effort to ensure a positive long-term recovery outcome, a professional who supports a patient's veganism *following* treatment should consider reasonably incorporating veganism into treatment itself. BALANCE Eating Disorder Treatment Center™, which accommodates vegan patients, addresses this with their goal to "include real world food exposures" as a part of a patient's treatment.

The recovered vegan and the recovered non-vegan can both feel equally free. An indicator of recovery is the extent of one's progress toward the goal of freedom around food. The vegan who (in a hypothetical case) worked just as hard as their non-vegan counterpart will not automatically be two steps behind them.

A person who is vegan can live as full and rich a life as their non-vegan friends. Just because someone is vegan does not mean they will not be sociable. The vegan person, like the non-vegan person, will come across situations in which they do not see appropriate options for themselves. This could happen for many reasons—allergies, location, finances, the time of day, the circumstances around the get-together. The recovered vegan can choose a vegan option if there is one as well as plan the day's meals around the known possibility of a non-vegan outing. (For example, on the way to a friend's informal wedding reception that I knew would serve non-vegan cupcakes, I bought myself a yummy red velvet cupcake beforehand and went on my merry way!) To someone who has obtained a level of eating disorder freedom, the idea of socializing might render dietary adaptation worthwhile. This is part of the flexibility inherent to recovery. Speaking to the dietary component of veganism alone, just as the person who is kosher, dairy-intolerant, or has celiac disease has the potential to recover, so does the person who is vegan. It stands to reason then that all eating disorder patients can and must be helped in figuring out their own way.

References

BALANCE Eating Disorder Treatment Center™. (n.d.). *Veganism, vegetarianism & kosher eating disorder recovery support*. Retrieved April 5, 2022, from https://balancedtx.com/veganism-vegetarianism-kosher-eating-disorder-recovery-support

Costin, C. (2007). *The eating disorder sourcebook: A comprehensive guide to the causes, treatments, and prevention of eating disorders*. McGraw-Hill.

Costin, C., & Grabb, G. S. (2012). *8 Keys to recovery from an eating disorder: Effective strategies from therapeutic practice and personal experience*. W.W. Norton & Co.

Hamilton, M. (2006). Disgust reactions to meat among ethically and health motivated vegetarians. *Ecology of Food and Nutrition, 45*(2), 125–158. https://doi.org/10.1080/03670240500530691

Henderson, Z. B., Fox, J., Trayner, P., & Wittkowski, A. (2019). Emotional development in eating disorders: A qualitative metasynthesis. *Clinical Psychology & Psychotherapy, 26*(4), 440–457. https://doi.org/10.1002/cpp.2365

Stanghellini, G., Castellini, G., Brogna, P., Faravelli, C., & Ricca, V. (2012). Identity and eating disorders (IDEA): A questionnaire evaluating identity and embodiment in eating disorder patients. *Psychopathology, 45*(3), 147–158. https://doi.org/10.1159/000330258

Stein, K. F., & Corte, C. (2006). Identity impairment and the eating disorders: Content and organization of the self-concept in women with anorexia nervosa and bulimia nervosa. *European Eating Disorders Review, 15*(1), 58–69. https://doi.org/10.1002/erv.726

The Vegan Society. *Definition of veganism.* www.vegansociety.com/go-vegan/definition-veganism.

Wolfram, T. (2019, August 9). *What does it mean to be an ethical vegan?* Taylor Wolfram. Retrieved April 8, 2022, from www.taylorwolfram.com/ethical-vegan/

7

VEGANISM'S TRAUMATIC ROOTS

Vegan eating disordered patients are unnecessarily impacted by eating disorder professionals' perceptions of veganism. When professional perceptions misguide treatment, patients must work that much harder to obtain the benefits that treatment aims to provide. Furthermore, if this unnecessary work goes unacknowledged by the treatment team, the vegan patient might need to bear it alone—the opposite of treatment's supportive aims.

The process of becoming vegan might feel traumatizing. Often, vegans have watched footage of animals living in deplorable conditions being abused, violated, and killed. They have watched animals express undeniable signs of physical and emotional pain. They have seen how animals, when separated prematurely from their family members, suffer. They have observed how animals are deprived of opportunities to behave in ways that are instinctual to them. Vegans who have seen these images have subsequently decided to stop contributing to the systems built on exploitation of animals for meat, dairy products, clothing, etc. Vegans

DOI: 10.4324/9781003310617-10

may have also had to come to terms with guilt about contributing to these systems in the past.

Vegan psychologist and author Clare Mann, BSc (Hons), MSc, MA, Post Grad Dip. COcc Psychol. AMAPS, FBPS, UKCP, created the term "vystopia" to describe this traumatic experience. "Vystopia," as defined in Mann's book, *Vystopia: The Anguish of Being Vegan in a Non-Vegan World*," is the "existential crisis experienced by vegans, arising out of an awareness of the trance-like collusion with a dystopian world and the awareness of the greed, ubiquitous animal exploitation, and speciesism in a modern dystopia" (Mann, 2018, p. 28). Feminist-vegan advocate, activist, and independent scholar Carol J. Adams defined "traumatic knowledge" as "the knowledge that a person has about the fate of the other animals" and explains that this causes "dissonance/disturbance/disjunction" (2018). In an International Association for Relational Psychoanalysis and Psychotherapy (IARPP) presentation, Dr. Shiri Raz defined the term "vegans' trauma" as:

> a chronic and complex trauma that can be described as a multi-layered trauma: A layer of vicarious trauma stemming from repeated exposure to animal suffering in our world, and a layer of a complicated, agonizing inter-relational and social trauma. Both layers influence each other, respectively the social and inter-relational.
>
> The social and inter-relational layer of the trauma is a result of society's contribution to the animals' trauma, which is their consumption habits of meat, fish, dairy and eggs, and its obliviousness to the vicarious traumatic stress it inflicts on vegans. (This) causes vegans to question their perception of reality and leaves them feeling isolated and hurt. (Raz, 2017).

According to Mann (2014), "For many, the images of animal abuse they have witnessed replay in their mind with flashbacks, nightmares and anger towards people who resist or deny what is happening to animals behind closed doors."

Anti-speciesism[1] Educator Dallas Rising—whose eating disorder recovery blog post will appear in Chapter 15—shares,

> The way I explain it to people is that, for many of us (vegans), we experience violence in spaces where others do not. When in the grocery store, we don't experience the "meat" aisle in the same way that carnists do. We see the bodies, blood, skin, and bones of individuals who lived lives of varying degrees of mutilation, manipulation, suffering, exploitation, and commodification only to be killed and dismembered for profit. Thus, vegans are much more likely to hold a lot of secondary trauma and that trauma is often triggered by what carnists view as food.
>
> (D. Rising, personal communication, March 24, 2022)

In Barbara McDonald's study about the process of going vegan (2000), she referred to the realization of this aforementioned knowledge as the "catalytic experience" (p. 8), which usually entailed "pain, shock, guilt, sadness, or depression" accompanied by "a cognitive interpretation that enabled the participant to immediately comprehend, as well as feel, the consequences of the new knowledge of animal abuse" (p. 9). Two of the 12 study participants experienced their catalytic event upon the re-emergence of formerly repressed information about animal cruelty (p. 10). Similar to a possible trauma response, "these participants put the information in the back of their minds until a later time, when another catalytic event facilitated its recall" (p. 6).

People Are Changed

The process of becoming vegan can change people. Findings from McDonald's study on this process revealed that "the vegans' transformed world views were shaped by a felt connection with non-human animals," of which "a central feature . . . was that animals were no longer viewed as

---

1 "The ethical concept that it is immoral to exploit or harm animals just because they belong to a different species" (Anti-speciesism.com, n.d.).

food," which in turn "became the foundation for an ethically-based praxis" (2000, p. 15). McDonald explained that, prior to becoming vegan, most of her participants' compassion for animals had "excluded food animals, because they did not see the connection between the animals they kept as pets and the animals they consumed as food" (p. 8). However, the study inevitably found "that the decision to be vegan . . . once made, was final" (p. 15).

The founder of Faunalytics, Che Green (2017), says, "As a new veg*n, you realize that animal suffering is everywhere, and that almost everyone you know is complicit." Relatedly, Rimaa Danielle Jomaa, MFT, RD (Psych Central, 2020), felt rage upon realizing "the crimes committed against nonhumans."

A new vegan might abruptly realize that they had been consuming what they now consider to be a product of grief. Adams (2018) says,

We are horrified, as we learn about the treatment of animals . . . We may feel revulsion at our own complicity. We have a need to forgive ourselves for our enmeshment within a system that daily destroys animals by the millions.

According to Krista Verrastro, MA, RDT (2019),

Vegans often experience a lot of sadness due to things such as: seeing constant reminders of cruelty and death . . . ; feeling excluded at work, family, and social events; feeling distant from significant others who aren't vegan; experiencing the struggles of raising vegan children; feeling powerless about the impact of meat and animal products on the environment; dealing with activist burnout.

According to Dr. Shiri Raz (personal communication, February 22, 2021), "In a world where animal use and abuse is ubiquitous, this emotional exposure gradually becomes a chronic and mentally painful experience which almost no one understands. It is a very lonely experience of pain."

Notably, the baseline reference for experiencing a traumatic response to animals' suffering is through indirect knowledge. The witnessing that Mann (2014) describes can just as easily refer to watching a video as it can to observing animals in person. Indeed, since becoming vegan a month prior to writing this on a public happycow.net forum, member Hippy_Han said,

> I . . . have watched so many documentaries and videos, read so many horror stories, seen pictures, read tweets and Facebook updates of animals being abused etc . . . basically I feel like my heart weighs a tonne and not a second goes by without an image flashing in my mind.

Additionally, a participant in McDonald's study who adopted veganism after watching a video on animal cruelty says of her experience, "The curtain was pulled back. The truth was made known. . . . It was like there is no turning back now. Now I know the cruelty that exists" (2000, p. 9). It is therefore reasonable to presume that viewing video content of animal cruelty might provoke a trauma response.

Now, let us consider a vegan person who, after learning about animal suffering, decided they wanted to help animals through pursuing activism. Perhaps this person's activism involved voluntarily "bearing witness" to animals in trucks as they enter slaughterhouses (Animal Save Movement) or entering factory farms and/or slaughterhouses themselves to capture undercover footage also intended for public view. Let us think how, in the latter case, the only way to obtain this footage was by going undercover. Let us think about what these activists have witnessed. Let us consider the trauma these activists might endure and the subsequent irreversible connection between their experience and its traumatic impact.

According to *Psychology & Veganism* author Apoorva Madan (2018):

> Following exposure to animal suffering, activists may go on to find themselves struggling to forget the graphic violence they witnessed, or the sensations they felt while they were there, having nightmares, or difficulties sleeping, noticing frequent feelings of anger and despair, unwanted memories of what they saw in the slaughterhouse each time they walk past the processed bodies of animals in the supermarket,

feeling distant and cut off from other people in their lives including friends or family, or holding beliefs that the world they live in is a horrible and unjust place.

Vegans have unequivocally equated the experience of cows, chickens, and all other animals deemed food to the experience of other animals deemed to be companions, such as dogs and cats. A vegan person considers that all animals should live and die in the way they either naturally would or in a way that is only done in their best interest (i.e., euthanizing a dog who is too sick to recover). McDonald notes of her study's participants that "typically, the vegan decision was made after a period of learning, in which the logical inconsistency of being in favor of animal rights but continuing to eat animal products was pondered" (2000, p. 14). Such learning necessarily comprises the realization that animals have personalities, families, instincts, emotions just like humans; that animals are sentient and vulnerable and want to live.

Vegans act from a place of believing that if animals could start a revolution, they would, but since they cannot, vegans have tried to do it for them. The revolution begins on their plates. Therefore, when a vegan is required to eat animals in eating disorder treatment, the freedom to do what they can in the interest of causing the least amount of harm to animals is stunted. The vegan's ability to take part in a movement that helps protect vulnerable beings is rendered useless.

References

Adams, C. J. (2018, April 30). *Traumatic knowledge and animal exploitation: Part 1: What—is it?* https://caroljadams.com/carol-adams-blog/traumatic-knowledge

Animal Save Movement. *Bearing witness.* https://thesavemovement.org/bearing-witness/

Anti-speciesism. (n.d.). *Antispeciesism.* Retrieved August 21, 2022, from https://anti-speciesism.com/anti-speciesism---our-definition.php

Dr. Raz, S. (2017). *The vegan's trauma.* The International Association for Relational Psychoanalysis and Psychotherapy.

Green, C. (2017, October 4). Evolution of a veg*n advocate. *Faunalytics.* https://faunalytics.org/evolution-vegn-advocate/

Jomaa, R. D. (2020, June 28). Four ways life as an animal activist taught me to change the world. *Psych Central*. https://psychcentral.com/blog/veganism/2020/06/four-ways-life-as-an-animal-activist-taught-me-to-change-the-world#1

Madan, A. (2018, February 25). PTSD and trauma in animal activists. *Psychology & Veganism*. https://animalandmind.com/2018/02/25/trauma-and-animal-activists/.

Mann, C. (2014, August 27). What strategies help vegans manage their trauma? *Vegan Psychologist—Clare Mann*. Retrieved April 4, 2022, from https://veganpsychologist.com/what-strategies-help-vegans-manage-their-trauma/

Mann, C. (2018). *Vystopia: The anguish of being vegan in a non-vegan world*. Communicate31 Pty Ltd.

McDonald, B. (2000). "Once you know something, you can't not know it". An empirical look at becoming vegan. *Society & Animals, 8*(1), 1–23. https://doi.org/10.1163/156853000x00011

Verrastro, K. (2019, September 30). *5 Ways to cope with sadness as a vegan*. MA RDT. www.kristaverrastro.com/5-ways-to-cope-as-a-vegan/

8

IMPLICATIONS OF NON-VEGAN EATING DISORDER TREATMENT

The process of becoming a vegan often fundamentally changes a person's worldview and concept of self, as discussed in the previous chapter. This intensely personal process may be devalued during eating disorder treatment if patients are not permitted vegan food. Requiring a person who has gone through this process to eat the very thing that they now consider a source of their own deep personal sadness, guilt, pain, and shame can prompt regression. What happens to the vegan whose positive process is subsequently thwarted?

Emily says,

> If I had been presented with the biggest, most high calorie, and "binge worthy" piece of vegan cake, even an entire cake, and told that I must eat it and I can't purge or I could eat one spoonful of fat-free, sugar-free, low-calorie dairy yogurt, I would eat the vegan food in a heartbeat. It's not even a question to me. I would eat ANYTHING before eating an animal product and I mean anything.

DOI: 10.4324/9781003310617-11

> Just like I wouldn't eat a dog, cat, or fellow human being, I would never eat an animal product from another fellow being, no matter what their species is.
>
> (Emily, personal communication, March 12, 2022)

Requiring a vegan person to eat animals means requiring them to further distort their relationship with food. Vegans have already made the connection that this piece of what everyone around them refers to as food was once a part of a living and breathing creature; they have already identified with the pain this creature invariably experienced; they have already brought into conscious awareness that "behind every meal of meat is an absence: the death of the animal whose place the meat takes" (Adams, 2015, p. xxiv). As a result of having rendered these realities conscious, Dr. Raz says, "The empathy we feel for the victims can cause us to suffer vicariously" (The International Association for Relational Psychoanalysis and Psychotherapy, 2017). Likewise, McDonald (2000), in whose study participants' "connectivity with nonhuman animals" upon transitioning to veganism "was made tangible by the animals' ability to feel pain"; additionally, "almost every participant mentioned the recognition of this close association with human feeling." Patients are being asked to deliberately return to a time in their minds that preceded a major developmental shift. For those who have undergone this process, being required to eat food they had eaten previously can feel traumatizing.

Emily's experience in treatment speaks to the heart of this need to hold onto one's own values. She shares,

> I started making bracelets with string and another patient taught me how to write my name in them by designing color coded patterns to create the lettering. After I learned how to do that, I realized that I could write anything. I made a green and purple bracelet with VERY thick lettering, reading "VEGAN" in all caps. I tied it to my wrist and quadruple knotted it. No one could tell me who I should be anymore. I might have been forced to eat animal products, but my heart was forever standing in solidarity with the animals. I made that bracelet as a symbol to myself that this hell would not be forever. That when I was discharged back home, that maybe just maybe, I could actually try to recover and keep

my body in a healthy place and eat a well-rounded vegan intake of food, instead of using food (even though it was vegan) to harm my body with and numb my emotions through binging and purging. This bracelet was my symbol of hope to myself and my symbol of apology and empathy to what the animals had gone through for their "by-products" to end up on my plate. A staff member came up to me and asked to see my bracelet. She read the word out loud "vegan . . ." and then looked at me. She had this angry look on her face like I was creating problems and being "disobedient." She got out a pair of scissors and told me that I needed to take it off. I demanded to know why and she said something about how it could trigger other patients and before I knew it, she snipped it off of my wrist with her scissors and said that she would return it to me before I'm discharged. I couldn't believe it!

(E., personal communication, March 12, 2022)

Mindfulness Versus Dissociation

Eating disorders may entail losing a sense of self. Consequently, recovery entails exploring one's own perspectives and applying those perspectives. This process can be immensely painful. If a clinician does not attend to a client's vegan-related pain, they may unintentionally prompt the client to get further away from—rather than more intimately connected to—themselves. However, recognizing that vegan-related trauma exists may present therapeutic material. Working with a patient through their feelings about living as a vegan and the process of becoming vegan might be what a vegan patient needs.

Eating disorder treatment involves developing a mindful presence with food. Patients are encouraged to identify and work through the source of negative feelings that they may be projecting onto food. According to Costin and Grabb,

Conscious eating is the ultimate goal for you and your relationship with food . . . . When you practice conscious eating you place an emphasis on awareness of your body signals, incorporate general education about nutrition, take into account any relevant health information, and eat the foods you truly enjoy.

(2012, p. 140)

For the full context, the authors go on to say that eating vegan as a means of being healthy in eating disorder recovery exists alongside other types of "nutritional mandates" and is "a rigid extreme." I want to make clear that I agree with the authors in viewing health motives this way but that I think ethical motivation is a separate category warranting a separate set of logic.

Eating disorder patients may use food to avoid connecting with their feelings by compartmentalizing food into mere nutritional components. Doing this ostensibly allows a person to make food the problem and thus also the solution. This provides a convenient rationale to keep the eating disorder going. It may feel quite effective in the short term, but of course, it is contributing to the progression of the disorder. There is a level of detachment that accompanies unyielding commitment to one's disorder.

Recovery, by contrast, prioritizes a mindful reconnection to both feelings and food. The recovering person may gradually welcome the sustenance that food provides them. They may become aware of the tastes and textures of food and experience joy when something tastes good. Eventually, they may regard the act of eating as a necessary and enjoyable part of living. The recovering person may first accept and then embrace their need for food.

A vegan person in eating disorder treatment may experience a specific type of detachment from food for reasons unrelated to their eating disorder. Eating disorder treatment implements the message that eating disorders are about more than food. However, a vegan eating non-vegan meals may find it impossible to focus on anything other than what they are having to eat. A vegan person may detach from their food because they are trying their hardest to detach from the fact that their food came from an animal. Feeding themselves may necessitate detachment.

Vegans' deepened awareness of what happens to animals in animal agriculture can make having to eat the products of that system feel traumatizing. Requiring vegans to eat the products of this system puts them in a position of having to somehow endure the eating process in the midst of their awareness that they are eating animals. During eating disorder treatment, vegans may need to disconnect from what they are eating. They may compartmentalize non-vegan food into its nutritional aspects alone so as not to connect with the whole of what is on their plate.

So while treatment aims to help patients see their food as more than just calories, vegans must enact the opposite in order to tolerate eating animals. Being put in a position that renders disconnection obligatory means being put in a position of making peace with the recovery process while denying their own ethics and beliefs. Emily, a vegan who has recovered from an eating disorder, says, "I was very focused on the food because I couldn't even attempt to enjoy the tastes because I knew what and who was behind it" (Emily, personal communication, March 12, 2022).

In disconnecting from their food, vegans are being asked to consciously do what Hamilton (2006, p. 156) claims meat-eaters unconsciously do to disconnect from their food's origins: "find meat problematic but cope with this by ignoring its origins or shielding themselves as much as possible against the realization of what it really is." Emily's perspective connotes Hamilton's perception of "meat as the product of violence towards sentient creatures," thereby rendering it an "object of ethical concern and conduct" as well as "an object of strong emotions involving disgust and horror" (Hamilton, 2006, p. 156). If patients often feel aversion to certain foods, then measures ought to be taken to identify the root cause of the aversion. This is because neglecting to do so or arriving at an inaccurate conclusion can cause harm.

I invite you to consider the following conceptualization of the non-vegan-to-vegan process: People in general regard violence toward animals by children as an undesirable behavior; it may even be an early symptom of sociopathy. We see how this behavior could lead to violence toward humans if not stopped. As a result, we would treat the child and help them relearn and develop compassion toward animals instead. The goal would be for them to never harm an animal again and to see what they did as wrong. Now, imagine telling an eating disorder patient who had a history of harming animals that part of their treatment entailed going back to harming animals; furthermore, that not doing so would be limiting their full recovery. I know this seems like a stretch, but it is essential to keep in mind that those who have undergone the process of becoming vegan consider their past consumption of animals as parallel to the child harming an animal while not knowing it was wrong. Or maybe even knowing it was wrong but not letting that stop them. The picture is crystal clear to a vegan that—in so many ways—they have inadvertently contributed to others harming animals on their behalf. Every time they purchased meat from the grocery store, the meat that they purchased was part of an animal who had been subjected to merciless violence before meeting their untimely end. As a result, vegans often need to make amends with themselves in order to progress in their lives.

Emily recounts,

> I would see the cheese and feel my heart drop into the pit of my stomach, imagining a mother cow being separated from her precious baby. I could viscerally feel the fear and panic, confusion, and devastation of the mother cow and her baby. Those feelings would then switch to extreme rage, as I imagined the farmer manhandling the innocent lives. I wanted to scream, kick, cry, and go up to that farmer and all of the others and yell so loud "LEAVE THEM ALONE!" as I could feel all of the dread that those animals must experience. Only for me, it was just in my imagination how they must feel. For the animals, it's real and that is their devastating reality. Every single meal and snack was hell on earth for this reason.
> (Emily, personal communication, March 12, 2022)

Imagine that the roles are reversed. This eating disordered vegan of whom we speak is, instead, an eating disordered meat eater. Imagine the extent of the meat eater's disorder is to the same degree as the vegan's. Consider the likelihood that, as a meat eater, the authenticity of the meat component of this person's diet would not be questioned, even though meat eaters would, just as vegans, be malnourished upon treatment admission. Consider the likelihood that they would get their meat-eating needs met without having to fight for them. Consider the likelihood that others might question whether they would really be eating meat if their brains were fully functional or whether their preference for meat could be clearly assessed. Consider the extent to which others might stop to wonder whether the meat eating was the disordered part and whether they actually wanted to be vegan. Consider the extent to which others might doubt that they were being true to themselves at their insistence on keeping meat in their diet. Consider the likelihood that others would question, caution against, or deny their choice. Then consider that when it comes to eating vegan—not restricting but just eating the vegan versions of animal food—the vegan choice is often questioned. The person who would rather eat mock meat than animal meat and is willing to face their eating disorder fear but not their revulsion to eating an animal is often questioned, doubted, and considered compromised by their eating disorder.

Emily shares,

> I ended up relapsing six years later and never went to treatment because I was so repulsed by the idea of my ethics and morals being taken from me again, so once I reached a point where I very likely could've been days away from dying, I summoned up everything in me to get myself physically well at home to avoid that added trauma in a treatment center. I ended up recovering completely on my own and I'm so grateful that I was able to do that, but with that being said, not everyone is able to do that and that's okay to need that extra help—but at what cost if you are an ethical vegan who only refuses the life-saving treatment because animal products would be forced upon them? This has to change!
>
> (Emily, personal communication, March 12, 2022)

Veganism is important to those who choose to adopt it because it is entrenched in the belief that harming animals is wrong. Mistrusting veganism can lead to a patient feeling personally mistrusted, which is unfortunate, considering that treatment should enliven self-trust. When veganism is conflated with this mistrust, when it is seen as either an extension of or a justification for their eating disorder, when it is clumped into the denial aspect of their eating disorder, treatment becomes a lot harder. Emily says,

> I had zero trust for my treatment team. I felt like they were on one team and I was on my own solo team of just myself. I felt like I was never truly able to address the issues behind my bulimia, let alone just express myself because all I could think about was the dread before every meal and snack because I wasn't eating "food." I was eating the suffering of others.
>
> (Emily, personal communication, March 12, 2022)

The potential lack of acknowledgment by a professional of a vegan's reaction to non-vegan meals could thwart a vegan patient's treatment. Not only might it prevent the real reasons for a vegan's discomfort from being recognized, but it also might detract from the real issues associated with the person's eating disorder.

A Vegan Patient's Unnecessary Work

Much of the recovery work that goes on for a vegan eating non-vegan meals involves the willful yet obligatory detachment from the food that is on their plate. The eating disorder treatment work is therefore rerouted to managing feelings around the non-vegan nature of their meals.

The importance of professional understanding here is paramount. In communicating awareness and empathy toward the vegan patient, professionals can directly lessen the amount of energy the person needs to channel toward eating non-vegan food. This understanding and support will allow the person's recovery status to accurately reflect the work they have put into recovery rather than reflect the energy left over after managing non-vegan food aversion. On the flip side, if the person does not receive that understanding, it is conceivable that they might progress insufficiently (and experience treatment-related ramifications compounding this insufficient progression, e.g., fewer privileges). The non-vegan meals could have played a role in limiting progress because the energy devoted to the vegan component of eating could have otherwise been spent on genuinely recovering. As with any issue that poses a potential barrier to effective treatment, this possibility ought to be recognized and adopted by treatment providers.

References

Adams, C. (2015). *Sexual politics of meat—25th anniversary edition—A feminist-vegetarian*. Bloomsbury Publishing Plc.

Costin, C., & Grabb, G. S. (2012). *8 Keys to recovery from an eating disorder: Effective strategies from therapeutic practice and personal experience*. W.W. Norton & Co.

Hamilton, M. (2006). Disgust reactions to meat among ethically and health motivated vegetarians. *Ecology of Food and Nutrition*, *45*(2), 125–158. https://doi.org/10.1080/03670240500530691

McDonald, B. (2000). "Once you know something, you can't not know it". An empirical look at becoming vegan. *Society & Animals*, *8*(1), 1–23. https://doi.org/10.1163/156853000x00011

Raz, S. (2017). *The vegan's trauma*. The International Association for Relational Psychoanalysis and Psychotherapy.

9

LOSING VEGANISM

We have explored how vegans, when confronted with non-vegan meals in treatment, risk having to grapple with an intolerable presence. Let us now shift our focus toward the experience of absence. Let us recognize that these individuals have lost their ability to eat vegan. Let us consider how the experience of this loss may play out for a vegan in non-vegan eating disorder treatment.

Food as Medicine

In eating disorder treatment, food is often viewed as akin to medicine. All kinds of food qualify as medicine—ranging from the most to the least nutritionally valuable. Since treatment encourages patients to recognize that food contains no moral value (a notion discussed in Chapter 6), the ability to eat a variety of foods on a consistent basis can be a marker of

DOI: 10.4324/9781003310617-12

eating disorder recovery progress. Consistently eating a variety of foods provides patients with nutrients to facilitate their healing along with practice at fostering a non-judgmental, non-restrictive mindset toward eating. Regarding food as medicine thus takes on both a literal and figurative meaning for the eating disorder patient.

I concur with the philosophy that food is medicine in eating disorder recovery. I also hold that its rationale warrants vegan-specific consideration. It is pivotal for professionals to understand that vegans may feel conflicted about the notion that non-vegan food is their medicine. If professionals make space for this possibility, they are better positioned to support vegan patients who struggle with using the "food as medicine" rationale as a means toward following treatment protocol.

I used the philosophy that food was medicine in my own eating disorder treatment. I thought that the eating disorder—a sickness—took my veganism from me; as a consequence, non-vegan food became my medicine. So it would stand to reason that eating non-vegan food would ultimately serve the purpose of getting myself and hence my veganism back. It was as though grieving veganism was an obligatory step toward recovery (even if that same recovery would ultimately lead me back to veganism). This is because eating disorder treatment connotes certain universally recognized consequences. Once you have taken the eating disorder client outside of their eating disorder's comfort zone, there is going to be massive discomfort.

However, the loss of eating vegan is not a natural consequence of having an eating disorder. To the contrary, recovery supposes a newly formed mistrust of the eating disorder. For one patient who says they are vegan, eating vegan may fall under the umbrella of eating disorder mistrust. For another patient who says they are vegan, eating vegan may not fall under the umbrella of eating disorder mistrust.

Losing the dietary component of veganism cannot be equated to losing an eating disordered based sense of safety or other unhealthful associations. The loss of vegan eating may instead involve a loss of felt identity and a loss of a healthful sense of security in the world.

In my case, veganism did not warrant inclusion in the list of "things my eating disorder took from me"—which, incidentally, is not the same thing as "things I was forced to give up due to eating disorder treatment." To that end, it can be said that treatment *itself* took veganism from me and that, by contrast, the loss of veganism's dietary component was decisively *not* my eating disorder's doing. Losing the dietary component of veganism put me in a position of having to grieve it.

My grief over veganism felt akin to four of Kubler's five grief stages: denial, anger, bargaining, and depression (Kubler-Ross & Kessler, 2005). I felt shocked due to the abruptness of the loss, sad due to the painful reconciliation of the loss, and angry due to my lack of power over the loss. I was even bargaining, i.e., "Once I recover, I'll get my veganism back."

Notably, I never reached the fifth grief stage, acceptance, because grieving veganism was neither natural nor inherent to my recovery. Grieving veganism was, for me, a markedly unnatural by-product of treatment itself—and grief's coinciding process was manufactured rather than allowed. Furthermore, nothing is gained in place of giving up vegan eating. It is not swapped for a better, more authentic, more lively aspect of recovery. It is only loss. It is a net negative.

Before I describe an experience below, I will highlight the following:

- The book's preface contains a disclaimer that this book is about older adolescents and adults. The following account is the single exception to this because: (a) I was given permission by the mother to include this vignette; (b) the mother made and supported the decisions outlined in the vignette; and (c) the experience described in this vignette may be generalizable regardless of age.
- I do not know how the daughter views the term "food as medicine."
- The mother from this vignette says, "My opinion is that anorexia can absolutely hijack veganism. I would argue that anything in a sufferer's life which is restrictive should be held up to the utmost scrutiny, including veganism."
- For clarity, the mother referenced below is anonymous. Eva Musby (2020), author of *Anorexia and Other Eating Disorders: How to Help Your Child Eat Well and Be Well*, shared the anonymous mother's post on her own website, anorexiafamily.com.

In recounting the experience of her vegan daughter being diagnosed with anorexia, an anonymous mother speaks of the difficulty in finding treatment. The mother looked for vegan treatment to no avail, remarking that treatment facilities "all said they would accommodate vegetarianism but not veganism," which the mother says "added a layer of uncertainty to what was already a horrifically stressful time" (Musby, 2020).

Due to the lack of vegan options and the need to admit her daughter to specialist eating disorder inpatient treatment as soon as possible, the mother chose a facility that she knew would not provide her daughter vegan food. Once this decision was made, her daughter "ceased to eat and drink completely." She then needed to be moved to a pediatric hospital ward where she was "placed on a nasogastric (NG) feed." However, the mother states that "in a hospital environment, [her daughter] saw food as medicine."

The mother describes how, over time, the hospital dietitian assessed her daughter's motivation, observed her ability to eat vegan foods even when the quantity was larger than fellow patients' non-vegan meals, and "sought guidance from other professionals . . . with expertise in eating disorders." By the conclusion of the daughter's treatment, the dietitian had determined that her "reasons for veganism were wholly ethical" and subsequently expressed her support of a vegan recovery upon discharge.

The vegan component of this situation worked out as well as it possibly could for the daughter. Her mother worked hard to admit her to a treatment center that would align with her values, ultimately making the necessary decision. The dietitian observed the daughter closely, asked colleagues questions, and ultimately aligned with the daughter's values in the best way she saw fit. While in treatment, the daughter was able to see food as medicine, which allowed her to get well. Getting well allowed her to realign with the dietary components of veganism once again.

Although this experience proved as ideal as possible given the associated limitations, I wonder—considering what we know about this vignette and about veganism—how treatment providers might consider supporting vegan patients in similar situations. If professionals find themselves in a similar position, they might ask themselves the following questions:

- Is there a possibility of reaching out to professional colleagues for guidance at an early stage of the patient's treatment, perhaps to help inform the nature of the initial assessment?
- Are there any alternative ways to assess for motivation early on, with the intention of reassessing as treatment progresses?
- To what extent is the patient emotionally affected by not having a vegan-only meal plan?
- Is there a way to gauge their level of vegan-specific hardship? What support/resources might help to assuage a portion of the vegan-specific emotional pain they may be experiencing?

Embodiment

In hindsight, I recognize that viewing my food as medicine was my way of coping with eating non-vegan food. It seemed unjust to me that my nutritional healing was a result of another being's demise; that pieces of another's body, by way of entering my own body, were contributing to my betterment. Likewise, from a vegan perspective, treatment's emphasis on developing healthy boundaries may feel contradictory to the blurring of boundaries between the body of the vegan and the body of the animal being eaten by the vegan—especially in the name of healing. This experience cannot be rationalized in vegan terms. If justified by a vegan patient, it is done so in spite of vegan values—not in harmony with them.

When I had anorexia, I thought that I had two primary goals. The first goal was to not gain weight, and the second goal was to lose weight. Not gaining weight was the very least my eating disorder could ask of me. Not gaining weight at least provided a protective barrier between things feeling in my control and things feeling entirely, dangerously, formlessly out of my control. Gaining weight meant that I had lost my anchor. It blurred the boundary between safe and unsafe. My body stopped feeling like a contained form. It overwhelmed me. Likewise, when I binged, I stopped feeling safe. The extent of my lack of containment was now limitless. If I could stay contained, I was controlling food and my body. If

I could not, then food and my body were controlling me. If I was being controlled, then I was completely at the mercy of something else. My world was small, but—according to my eating disorder—it was mine. As soon as I crossed that boundary, I blurred with forces outside of my control, and suddenly, the potential for continued loss of agency became limitless. There was no proverbial ceiling.

It is therefore worth considering the following questions to better understand a vegan's experience of embodiment and boundaries: How does eating part of an animal's body impact the vegan's experience of their own body? How does digesting the remnants of what was once alive impact the vegan's experience of their own body? What sorts of attachment issues might the vegan person—understandably—be projecting onto the animal they are made to eat? What process does the vegan person undergo knowing they must eat the animal, seeing the animal in front of them, putting part of the animal into their mouth, and then digesting this animal part?

Professionals are responsible for keeping in mind the potential for traumatic experiences at every point along the way during treatment. From a vegan perspective, none of these trauma reactions are unreasonable. Replace "meat" with "dog," "cat," "horse," "gerbil," "guinea pig," and "rabbit" and you might get a sense of the vegan person's visceral experience of eating meat from a cow or a pig. Oliver (2021, p. 4), says, "The boundaries of the body are permeable, constituted beyond us . . . whose body does my body consume to sustain me? In what processes and spaces am I implicated by eating these bodies?" To what extent, then, is a lack of permission to eat vegan presenting a barrier to that which played an integral role in reconciliation of eating disorder–related issues?

Defenses

Eating disordered clients are understandably positioned to forgo their coping mechanisms—in this case, their eating disordered behaviors. Including veganism in the category of restrictive behaviors is essentially grouping it in with eating disordered coping mechanisms. For a true vegan, it is obviously not a coping mechanism but rather an ethical decision. Treating it like a coping mechanism poses a risk of interfering with a healthy mindset, the mindset that actually belongs to the person rather than the eating disorder. Professionals must recognize the potential for this risk when concluding that a person's veganism is eating disordered in nature. When vegan eating is wrongfully assumed to be restriction and thus discouraged or unpermitted, the healthy part of that person is not fostered. The part of the person that may have actually served a purpose in their recovery has been devalued. This is concerning because treatment aims to do the *opposite* of devaluing patients.

Loss of Identity

Related to the loss of this possible coping mechanism is the loss of identity. When someone enters treatment, it is expected that they will do their best to forgo all eating disorder behaviors to the best of their ability. The expectation is not to force the person to recover fully, but to minimize the behaviors as much as possible so that the person has a chance at unconditionally full recovery. This recovery cannot happen if eating disorder behaviors are still occurring. Recovery is a potentially long haul, and providers recognize that stabilizing behaviors is only the first stage. But in order to have that full recovery, behavioral stabilization becomes non-negotiable. One of the problems here, however, is that oftentimes, eating disorder patients identify with their eating disordered behaviors and may forget who they are without them. So when the behaviors are taken away, it can leave patients very raw and vulnerable. This speaks even more strongly to the point that patients need support as they forgo this supposed aspect of their identity.

A vegan person, when not permitted to eat vegan in eating disorder treatment, in a sense is giving up two identities at once. Because that eating disorder identity feels real in its own right, it doesn't fully matter that it isn't a "real" identity. It is still being forgone, and a grieving process often ensues (Center for Discovery, n.d.; Nussbaum, 2022). However, a vegan identity is also taken away when veganism is not permitted.

Who am I without my eating disorder? This is a question I have heard asked and a question that I myself have asked. The answer to this question might feel out of reach, especially early on in recovery. However, veganism could be one way for an eating disordered person to easily recall a part of their authentic self. Certainly, McDonald's (2000) study (discussed in Chapter 7) indicated that "the process of learning to become vegan was rooted in the individual's sense of who they are and how they fit in the world" (p. 5). If veganism is something that a client feels makes them who they are, then they need support to preserve that part of themselves as much as possible, especially upon having to forgo veganism's dietary component.

Comorbid Trauma

Let us also consider instances where someone's vegan-related trauma ties into prior personal trauma. Issues around unhealthy attachment may contribute to the onset of eating disorders (Gander et al., 2015). Perhaps a patient with a history of loss and detachment felt moved to choose veganism upon learning about the familial detachment experienced by animals raised for food. Indeed, according to Taft (2016, Kindle location 1172),

> Many animal advocates have personally experienced trauma themselves. In fact, for many of us, our personal experiences of abuse and injustice are what have helped us develop the mindset that we must fight to prevent all vulnerable creatures from experiencing unnecessary trauma and abuse.

By extension, I wonder if veganism might offer some people a legitimate means toward mending or healthfully channeling the impacts of past trauma. We should thus consider whether taking away a person's option to eat vegan will simultaneously take away the mechanism that profoundly aided their trauma recovery. In my opinion, failing to recognize (and, by extension, failing to dignify) the relationship between veganism and trauma recovery can pose a risk to a person's well-being. When a vegan person is required to stop eating vegan foods in eating disorder recovery, it is possible that they will become retraumatized. If that person is in a facility that is not primarily equipped to treat both eating disorders and trauma, this can set the stage for profound harm that could have been avoided.

Considering the aforementioned themes that may arise in certain vegan eating disorder patients, eating disorder professionals might become curious about the following questions: What about a patient who became vegan because of the empathy they felt upon discovering the parent-child separation integral to the process of raising animals for food? What about a patient whose discovery of animals' plights might have connected with their own developmental attachment issues? What about a patient for whom veganism is connected to issues regarding instinctual needs—or any needs—being neglected or mishandled? What about a patient whose veganism ties into issues around their very personhood or identity being neglected or mishandled? To what extent did a patient's unmet needs play a part in the development of their eating disorder? To what extent did veganism offer reconciliation of past issues that contributed to their eating disorder?

A vegan person in eating disorder treatment who loses the ability to eat vegan food is going to be affected by this loss. Each vegan person will be affected differently, but this loss is one that warrants professional vegan-specific understanding and support. This person is not just losing an aspect of their eating disorder—a loss that comes with its own uniquely understandable reaction. This person is also losing an aspect of what makes them who they are and how they have authentically developed. The process of going vegan as discussed in Chapter 8 is often intense and life altering. Patients in this position may need their treatment professionals to support them in processing this loss.

References

Center for Discovery Blog. *Coping with the loss of yourself during eating disorder recovery.* https://centerfordiscovery.com/blog/coping-loss-eating-disorder-recovery/

Gander, M., Sevecke, K., & Buchheim, A. (2015). Eating disorders in adolescence: Attachment issues from a developmental perspective. *Frontiers in Psychology*, 6. https://doi.org/10.3389/fpsyg.2015.01136

Kübler-Ross, E., & Kessler, D. (2005). *On grief & grieving: Finding the meaning of grief through the five stages of loss.* Simon & Schuster.

McDonald, B. (2000). "Once You Know Something, You Can't Not Know It" An empirical look at becoming vegan. *Society & Animals, 8*(1), 1–23. https://doi.org/10.1163/156853000x00011

Musby, E. (2020, September 5). *Is it OK for my child to be vegan during eating disorder treatment?* Eva Musby. https://anorexiafamily.com/vegan-eating-disorder/.

Nussbaum, A. (2022, January 21). *Dealing with a feeling of identity loss in eating disorder recovery.* BALANCE Eating Disorder Treatment Center™. Retrieved April 3, 2022, from https://balancedtx.com/blog/dealing-with-a-feeling-of-identity-loss-in-eating-disorder-recovery

Oliver, C. (2021). Vegan world-making in meat-centric society: The embodied geographies of veganism. *Social & Cultural Geography.* https://doi.org/10.1080/14649365.2021.1975164

Taft, C. (2016, March 19). *Trauma in animal advocacy.* Vegan Publishers. https://veganpublishers.com/trauma/.

10

ANIMAL THERAPY IN NON-VEGAN EATING DISORDER TREATMENT

Animal therapy often has a positive impact on an eating disordered individual's treatment. I have personally witnessed the meaningful effects that therapy dogs have had. Dogs' inclusion in people's care never ceases to warm me. I am pleased that therapy animals are, at times, part of a recovering person's treatment process. However, the inclusion of animal therapy in an eating disorder patient's treatment protocol necessitates discussion in the context of veganism.

Animal therapy experts have vouched for its tangible effects. For example, according to Levinson (1984, abstract), an animal can serve "a) as a psychotherapeutic adjunct, b) as the sole therapist, c) as a catalytic agent for change, d) as a means of contact with nature, one's unconscious and the universe." Additionally, Chandler (2017, p. 233), in discussing an equine activity intending to improve both self-reflection and communication with others, suggests that:

DOI: 10.4324/9781003310617-13

the horse–human relationship has the opportunity to be strengthened during several interactive equine activities that take place over the course of treatment, and the relationship flourishes in an environment of support and honesty that benefits both the individual and the group.

Chandler also asserts,

It is easy to predict how a dog feels about being approached or interacted with because it tends not to hide its feelings. Thus, people can feel more comfortable being able to understand the animal's behavior when around them. Therapy dogs like just about everyone, so clients can feel immediate, genuine acceptance the moment they enter the counseling room.

(2017, p. 74)

Moreover, clinical observation of the relationship between patients and animals can help therapists more accurately assess how to support their patients as, according to Chandler (2017, p. 105), "If we can accurately interpret signals of an animal's perception of clients' emotional and attitudinal states, then we have significantly more information about our clients with which to understand them better and to assist them."

Some treatment centers that caution against veganism incorporate animal therapy into their treatment protocol. This simultaneous implementation of animal therapy and vegan eating may be perceived by a vegan as a demonstrable disconnection between animals whose *aliveness* is meant to heal and animals whose *inanimateness* is meant to heal. It pains a vegan to realize day in and day out that dogs are regarded as pets and cows are food, as this connection likely had something to do with why they became vegan in the first place. Being told of the healing benefits of animals while being made to eat animals can feel like betrayal to a vegan.

Most vegans will have recognized the healing power of bonding with animals before becoming vegan. They recognize that animals are perfect just as they are, rendering their mere presence healing. They recognize that animals need do nothing to be loved; that they can be loved for their very nature and recognized as whole, beautiful, precious creatures.

A friend of mine, Reverend Glen Ganaway, speaks to this concept beautifully, saying,

> Every cat is born knowing how to be a cat. And we recognize each cat, no matter its color or size, as a cat. And we appreciate the catness of the cat. NO Matter the CAT. We have an inner nature that loves and cares for us, just as we are. BECAUSE we are the way we are and live and think as we do.
> (G. Ganaway, personal communication, April 4, 2022)

This is the very recognition that led vegans to believe animals are worthy of living freely, the very recognition that led vegans to regard an animal as someone. In a vegan's mind, the cow, the horse, and the dog are all on the same level. All retain equal inherent value. The entire vegan journey consists of developing an understanding that there is no inherent difference between animals we call food and animals we call companions. So while animal therapy ought to be a meaningful and connective experience, a vegan may have a hard time being fully present, knowing all the while that this same center is about to serve them a different type of animal for a meal.

Along those lines, it is noteworthy that "possible therapy animals include pocket pets (such as hamsters), rabbits, reptiles, llamas, dolphins, . . . cats, . . . dogs and horses" (Meyers, 2017). All of these animals surely contain similar nutrients to their food animal counterparts, but treatment centers do not consider them essential toward meeting patients' needs and are thus not serving them to patients. While it is true that treatment centers attempt to model regular life and thus would have no reason to serve these particular animals, we must still regard this dichotomy through a vegan lens. Regardless of the reasoning for serving one animal over another, vegans register the distinction. Vegans may find this distinction disconcerting; hence the importance of recognizing the particular support that a vegan in eating disorder treatment may warrant.

As a recovered person who is vegan, I am acutely aware of when those around me with dogs are eating other animals. This awareness causes me to feel pain. However, unlike my time as a vegan patient receiving eating disorder treatment, I do not have to cope with this pain by tuning out reality because I can eat food in alignment with those same values that are dictating my unrest at seeing the meat-eating dog owner. The only thing—the only thing—that can make it any better in the moment is knowing that I have the freedom to choose veganism, that I have chosen this way of life that allows me to see the cow and the dog as equal. It is the knowing of myself that alleviates the depth of that suffering, the knowledge that I have chosen and continue to choose in alignment with my values. But yes, even today, as a recovered person, I get upset; I feel pained; I feel frustrated, angry and defeated sometimes.

Also, I am recovered. I am not in my eating disordered mind. Yet, even today, as someone who has the choice to eat vegan and who makes that choice with everything I consume, and for whom connection with that veganism is the path out of the anguish I feel at the sight of someone with a dog eating an animal, I still feel the anguish. It comes, and I work through it in accordance with my values; my values are the key to working through it. During my eating disorder treatment, the lack of ability to act upon my values hurt me. My eating disorder made it worse because it would have highlighted for me just how little autonomy I had. This is what I mean when I speak in Chapter 9 of the risks in taking something away that is not part of the eating disorder. The removal of something that brings a healthy sense of safety—something that is experienced as a healthy reconciliation—can result in the known detrimental effects of that which the patient may experience as forced regression.

The benefits of therapy animals' company are evident in observing their sensitivity to human behavior. This is because they are "excellent distress detectors," according to Cynthia Chandler, director of the Consortium for Animal Assisted Therapy at the University of North Texas, as expressed by the horse "moving toward an anxious client to soothe the person or moving away when the situation feels overwhelming to them" (Meyers, 2017).

Vegans are conscious of the fact that animals considered to be food are equally good at detecting distress as their "therapy animal" counterparts; so good in fact that, when it comes to their own and their families' distress, they react in the same way these horses would if they too were being harmed or aware of their families' harm. However, in the former scenario, we work with the horses on the horses' terms, according to their nature, to help facilitate healing via their sentience. We therapeutically utilize their intuitiveness, ability to feel psychological anguish, and ability to pick up on the anxiety of others. We recognize that an inherent part of the therapeutic benefit is that the horse stays intact. Not only do we recognize that the horse ought not be harmed, but we also acknowledge that the horse should be shown love and care. It is the love and care shown to the horse—the appreciation of the horse being alive, present, sentient, sensitive, receptive—that facilitates our healing. We rely on those aspects of the horse and would not dare tamper with them. However, when it comes to animals as food, we require that they be used, exploited, abused, disregarded, and perceived as inanimate. We see them as sources of nutrition for ourselves, completely separate from the beings they once were, that is: sentient beings worthy of our utmost respect, just like our equine and canine friends.

I understand that treatment centers have pure intentions with animal therapy. However, at the very baseline, I deem it important to foster increased understanding of the vegan experience so as to allow for the most optimal treatment of a vegan person in this situation. Optimal treatment, while not automatically synonymous with allowance of vegan eating, is automatically synonymous with helping a patient feel valued, understood, and supported to the best of one's ability.

The discussion of animal therapy in a vegan's eating disorder treatment fosters an understanding of what veganism is, why it matters, how alignment with its values can be highlighted, and what it specifically means to a vegan in recovery.

Vegans are aware of this species-related cognitive dissonance. As a result, the vegan person in this treatment setting is essentially observing a setting simultaneously holding two opposite actions—each in the name of recovery—in equal regard: firstly, the *eating* of *some* kinds of animals and, secondly, the *connecting* with *other* kinds of animals. The vegan here must reconcile their knowledge that a treatment center whose protocol necessitates *oblivion* of *one* animal's former sentience in order to eat that animal also necessitates *appreciation* of *another* animal's current sentience in order to *bond* with that animal. It is implied that patients remain unconscious of the former while facilitating consciousness of the latter.

As a result, the vegan is positioned to reconcile what they *must* do versus what they feel they *could never* do—all in the name of getting better.

The vegan here must reconcile that the same treatment center demonstrating a love for animals is also demonstrating a passivity when it comes to animals having been harmed. They are acutely aware that the treatment center is a safe haven for the horses versus a morgue for the cows; a place where horses have arrived safely at their destination, their home, where they are (ideally) cared for and protected, while cows who have arrived at the same destination have done so in the aftermath of slaughter. Vegans register this on a conscious level. Try to imagine yourself in a situation that is reversed. The cow is the therapy animal and the horse is the meal. You might form a connection with the cow and go inside for a meal to eat the remains of a cooked horse. If you can imagine that for even an instant, then you can imagine a fraction of the vegan's experience. Vegans face this reconciliation with every meal as it is, but when presented with an animal whose aliveness is celebrated, there is greater work to be done in the name of reconciliation—and recovery.

Also, because veganism is concerned with animal mistreatment, vegans may have concerns about the therapy animal's well-being. For example, vegans might wonder whether the animal is in any way being harmed by the experience, where the animal lives when not in the therapeutic setting, and how the animals are obtained, e.g., whether they are rescued or purchased. If purchased, the vegan patient might wonder whether the purchase helps to maintain an exploitative industry. All of these concerns are valid within the context of veganism.

Perhaps the patient does not feel like they can ask these questions, or perhaps the questions, for any number of reasons, cannot be answered. Perhaps the patient finds out that the answers to these questions confirm their worries. For these reasons, concern over a therapy animal's well-being may compromise a patient's treatment. Much like the previously discussed eating of meat at the treatment table, here, the patient would be betraying their own values by attempting to see their reality differently—a prospect incompatible with full recovery.

References

Chandler, C. K. (2017). *Animal-assisted therapy in counseling* (3rd ed.). Routledge. https://doi.org/10.4324/9781315673042

Levinson, B. M. (1984). Human/companion animal therapy. *Journal of Contemporary Psychotherapy*, *14*, 131–144. https://doi.org/10.1007/BF00946311 (for some reason the identical link in the text went to a different article).

Meyers, L. (2017, December 26). The people whisperers. *Counseling Today*. https://ct.counseling.org/2017/12/the-people-whisperers/.

11

IDENTITY

While eating disorders and veganism fall into separate groups, within each of these groups lies a range of experiences and beliefs. We may consider perceiving individuals within each group through an "emic" lens, which is "the insider or subjective viewpoint" that "emphasizes ideas and members' perceptions and interpretations of events, behaviors, relationships, and other phenomena of interest to the group or community" (Wilson, 2005, p. 19).

Vegan Individual Differences

While the term "veganism" is clearly defined, beyond sharing a value system, "vegans" may differ vastly from one another—both in the way they practice veganism and in the complexity of who they are as individual people. Veganism means a shared value system but beyond that, vegans can differ from one another in countless ways—personality, location, race, ethnicity, age, gender, religion, occupation, relationship status, parental status, etc.

DOI: 10.4324/9781003310617-14

Are they driven toward activism and, if so, how? Have they experienced vegan-related trauma? How long have they been vegan? Do they identify with other vegans? Do they feel they belong to a vegan community? Do they claim the label "vegan" for themselves? Do they consider veganism a part of their identity? Were they raised vegan? Is anyone in their family vegan? How closely do they identify with the various aspects of veganism? Do they consider it ethical to purchase secondhand leather? Many vegans draw a line in the sand at different points. There are many issues on which not all vegans see eye to eye. There is plenty of room for discourse within the vegan community itself.

Vegan Identification

Different vegan individuals may adopt the identity of veganism to varying degrees. Some are very open about it, and some are more private. Some explicitly call themselves vegan, and others, while living according to vegan ethics, do not label themselves as vegan. Some vegans identify as vegan as a part of their work (e.g., working at a vegan restaurant) or advocacy (e.g., a representative of a vegan organization). The degree to which a vegan person adopts the identity of veganism may change over time. A 2021 study by Judge et al., that considered how the social identity of vegans influenced vegan activism found differences between "deontological" and "consequentialist" orientations among vegans (p. 3). Activism of vegans with a deontological orientation was indirectly associated with "anger," while activism of vegans with a consequential orientation was not (p. 7). Activism of vegans with a deontological orientation was indirectly associated with "identification with vegans" and "identification with animals and group efficacy," while activism of vegans with a consequentialist orientation was indirectly associated with either "identification with animals" or "identification with vegans" (p. 7). No matter the differences among individual vegans' identification, it is important to remember that the vegan person is constantly aligned with vegan ethics, even in situations in which limitations restrict their ability to act according to these values, such as in non-vegan eating disorder treatment.

Eating Disorder Individual Differences

Likewise, those with eating disorders can differ in countless ways from one another—not only on the obvious level of the type of eating disorder they may have, but also how that particular eating disorder plays out in their lives. There are differences in the kind of toll the eating disorder takes on their psychological health, their physical health, how "sick" society perceives them to be, how sick they perceive themselves to be, what they regard as being "sick enough," and their relationship with their physical body as they exist in the world (including their size, etc.).

And that just concerns the eating disorder itself. Eating disordered individuals have histories and lives comprised of countless non–eating disordered elements. And these lives are as unique as the individual living them. As with veganism, there are differences in gender, age, religion, race, ethnicity, relationship status, family status, etc. How isolated do they feel? Where do they live? What do they do for work? How do any of these factors influence their feelings about recovery?

Eating Disordered Identification

Eating disordered individuals, on the whole, have a different type of relationship to an eating disorder identity than vegans have to a vegan identity. The criteria for establishing an eating disorder identity is formulated by a distorted perception of themselves. If there is ownership of this identity, it implies a level of instability. The eating disorder identity may be real, but it is also unreliable and unstable. The individual protects their distorted self-image via eating disordered behaviors; however, this apparent protective mechanism simultaneously causes mental and physical damage. A recovery goal for an eating disordered person is to not identify with their eating disorder.

However, much like the differences among individual vegans' interpretations of a vegan identity, eating disordered individuals can differ from one another in terms of how they identify with their eating disorder. Different individuals with eating disorders may identify with their eating disorders in different ways. Among eating disordered individuals, there are individual-specific varieties of ego-syntonic behaviors, which the person regards as "part of themselves," and ego-dystonic behaviors, which the person regards as "separate from themselves" (Aspen et al., 2014, p. 1), or, as Purcell Lalonde et al. research found, a "fear of self" (2015, p. 179). Moreover, the ego-syntonic/dystonic behavior variety may render one's eating disorder identity ambiguous.

Intersection of the Two Groups

Let us consider that the eating disorder group and the vegan group are, in fact, separate groups, each complete with its own definition, criteria, meaning, roots, motivation, and aims. Each group operates along its own continuum. We may consider perceiving these group differences through an "etic" lens, which is "the outsider or objective viewpoint" (Wilson, 2005, p. 19).

Sometimes the continuums intersect. Now, the thesis statement of this book—the nugget of information that needs to underlie all other information—is that the moment these groups intersect is the moment veganism stops being an issue in its own right. Instead of bringing veganism's supposedly negative impact to the fore, the intersection should cue us to reframe our perception of the person's eating disorder. The veil has been pulled back. The jig is up. *We see you, eating disorder trickster. We see what you've been doing to this person to justify subsisting in their brain. We're onto you.*

I think if it were me, I'd be mad at my eating disorder. I'd want to say, *Wow, you've gone to such great lengths to try to make me feel guilty about eating a non-vegan diet. You've messed with me in such a way that now if I eat non-vegan again, you've set me up to feel like a less compassionate person. You've set me up to make me feel like I've abandoned a moral code. Well, screw you, eating disorder! Who are you to set any moral codes in the name of any cause?! I don't think you should be the one blabbering on about morals, eating disorder, when I'm only getting sicker at the hands of your supposed moral authority.*

An eating disordered person who realizes they were never vegan in the first place might as well be realizing that they were never a Jim Jones fan in the first place. It makes no difference. Veganism is just an accessible term for the eating disorder to latch onto in the name of making rules. Any rules in the name of maintaining an eating disorder are destructive, point blank period.

But here's the kicker:

Eating disorder rules are arbitrary.
Vegan rules are not.

So an eating disordered person will latch onto one supposed system as easily as they might latch onto another. The existence of rules matters more than any objective logic behind those rules. Replace the rule of "only eat the vegan version of cheese" with "only eat bananas after 2 p.m."; replace "eat the vegan chocolate chip cookie" with "eat pancakes in solitude but waffles with others"; replace "get the mock deli meat" with "eat chickpeas with a fork." It's all arbitrary. It doesn't make sense. It's a system that the eating disordered voice devised in order to mess with the innocent person in its grip.

Also, there is a sizeable difference between eating disorder rules and vegan "rules," which are not so much rules as they are guidelines. Unlike eating disorders, if a vegan person accidentally eats a non-vegan food, there is no compensatory punishment; no metaphorical death by hell-fire; no proverbial Hail Marys; no tightening of the reins to such a degree that the person can no longer move. That isn't to say the vegan wouldn't feel badly, but it isn't a self-punishing type of badness. If a vegan person breaks the "rules," they react as a *vegan* would, not as an *eating disordered person* would. Vegans may have an array of reactions, but all pertaining to the literal act of having just eaten something non-vegan. Once the moment has passed, oftentimes, they will feel better. It's not something that inherently festers or nags. It might for a little while, and they might need to talk about it to other vegans who understand, but the issue itself begins and ends with that one oversight. It isn't deeper; it isn't a reflection of the self; it isn't grounds to spiral. An ethically vegan person would not say, "Screw this, I messed up once, so I'm throwing in the vegan towel." That wouldn't happen. An eating disordered person, on the other hand, may very well respond in this manner to breaking an eating disordered rule.

These are two different experiences, each with a mentality and trajectory all its own. So an overlap of the two does not imply that one has magic-ally morphed into the other. Rather, if veganism turns out to be an eating disordered guise, the reality that it was an eating disorder all along simply comes into the light. No guilt, no shame. The issue simply isn't veganism. The issue is the eating disorder, and the information coming to light is how the eating disorder has been manifesting itself.

Oftentimes, this issue is not clear-cut. There is confusion. The person might strongly align with animal ethics, which may account for their vegan choices. *And* they might have an eating disorder. *And* they might have difficulty defining a line where their vegan choices belong in the vegan category and their eating disorder symptoms belong in the eating disorder category. This confusion is valid, which is why individualized, ongoing assessment is imperative. However, it is important to recognize basic distinctions between the two concepts when encountering a blurred version of each. Even in the blurriest of circumstances, the eating disorder is still the eating disorder and veganism is still veganism. And the eating disorder identity, by its very nature, is still *inauthentic* to who the person is, whereas the vegan identity, by its very nature, is still *authentic* to who the person is. Should the label of veganism fall into the eating disorder category, it is still the *eating disorder* that is inauthentic—not *veganism*. The part of veganism that belongs to the eating disorder is automatically inauthentic.

Identity, no matter what it involves, is an important part of eating disorder recovery. An eating disorder can seem to strip a person of who they once were, what matters to them, and how they assert themselves in the world. It can seem to completely blindside their goals and passions. It can seem to all but replace their personality. The toll that repeated, long-term eating disorder behaviors take on the body and mind is very real. Sense of self is thwarted. Personally, I was numb much of the time. I was disconnected from my own core. I could not assert myself in the world because I had lost myself. My emotional experiences were centered around my eating disorder–related thoughts and behaviors. An eating disorder redesigns the structure of a person's world. It's like living in a home for so many years, and suddenly your home becomes an Escher painting. You don't even know where the front door is.

So yes, finding yourself again is a defining marker of recovery. Being able to assert who you are and who you aren't—and believe yourself as you're doing so—is integral to the recovery process. And for a vegan eating disordered person, this identification may or may not be clear-cut. But because aligning with one's true self is so essential to recovery, helping a vegan person know and trust their true vegan identity really, really matters.

Eugene Gendlin (1996, Kindle location 3995–3997) coined the term "life-forward movement" in asking,

> What might it be that points 'toward more life'? It might be to let oneself have feelings (if they have been blocked), or to assert one's own perceptions (if one has long discounted them). It might be to say something one has long felt but not said. It might be to permit oneself to feel a little bit of hope.

Indeed, helping the vegan person who truly aligns with vegan values assert themselves as a vegan can move their recovery forward because it moves them forward.

References

Aspen, V., Darcy, A. M., & Lock, J. L. (2014). Patient resistance in eating disorders. *Psychiatric Times*. Retrieved April 7, 2022, from www.psychiatrictimes.com/view/patient-resistance-eating-disorders

Gendlin, E. T. (1996). *Focusing-oriented psychotherapy a manual of the experiential method*. The Guilford Press.

Judge, M., Fernando, J. W., & Begeny, C. T. (2022). Dietary behaviour as a form of collective action: A social identity model of vegan activism. *Appetite, 168*, 105730. https://doi.org/10.1016/j.appet.2021.105730

Purcell Lalonde, M., O'Connor, K., Aardema, F., & Coelho, J. S. (2015). Food for thought: Ego-dystonicity and fear of self in eating disorders. *European Eating Disorders Review, 23*(3), 179–184. https://doi.org/10.1002/erv.2349

Wilson, T. D. (2005, May 28). Participant observation. *Encyclopedia of Social Measurement*. Retrieved April 8, 2022, from www.sciencedirect.com/science/article/pii/B0123693985003984?via%3Dihub

Section III

A WAY FORWARD

As I said in the introduction to Section II, perspectives on vegans and eating disorder treatment must be talked about. Neglecting to talk about them leads us to not being equipped or ready to support vegan eating disordered individuals. So here we are, we've talked about this situation, and now we can shift our focus to proactive professional movement. This section explores professional movement forward via assessments, treatment approaches and principles, and internal professional work. It culminates in the positing of a "vegan-informed" model, adapted from the trauma-informed model, so that we have a map, a framework. Within such a framework, concepts in this book are given a home, a point of reference—one that is individualized and adaptable, as has been emphasized thus far.

DOI: 10.4324/9781003310617-15

12

PROFESSIONALLY CONSIDERING A PATIENT'S VEGANISM

How might we consider the circumstances under which a patient is permitted to eat vegan in eating disorder recovery? How might nuance factor into these considerations? Getting to the root of a patient's needs can give rise to an understanding of what their veganism *is* or *is not* as well as how their vegan diet *does* or *does not* serve them.

In accordance with these considerations, various assessment ideas and approaches have been suggested by professionals. These suggestions may serve as clinical guides toward viewing patients holistically and, in doing so, allow patients to experience themselves as proactive partners in their own treatment. Below are several ideas and approaches used by eating disorder treatment professionals.

Tammy Beasley, MS, RDN, CEDS-S, LD, regards clients whose intentions are rooted in ethics but whose eating disorders led them astray as akin to having "worthy intentions behind riding their bicycle but sometimes [struggling] in their relationship with biking

DOI: 10.4324/9781003310617-16

or exercise." Alternatively, the distinction becomes concerning to Beasley "when the food belief has robbed an individual of variety, spontaneity, relationships, flexibility, and daily nourishment to thrive."

(Beasley, 2020)

Founder and CEO of BALANCE Eating Disorder Treatment Center™ Melainie Rogers MS, RDN, CDN, CED-S, encourages patients "to openly reflect on the reasons for choosing to follow this dietary pattern" and assures prospective patients that their treatment team will work with them "to assess these motivations throughout treatment" (2019). Even if it has been decided initially that eating vegan can work, continual exploration of nuance—as opposed to merely checking the "allowance-to-eat-vegan-box"—can help a patient make the most of their recovery process both during and after treatment. The process should be a mutually conscious iteration that the patient's well-being takes precedence.

In following with their perspectives, Beasley and Rogers co-created the "Separating My Food Beliefs from My Eating Disorder" questionnaire (Figure 12), intended for broad use:

Separating My Food Beliefs from My Eating Disorder

1. When did your eating disorder behaviors first begin?

2. How long have you been following a vegan meal plan?

3. What other lifestyle changes have you made to accommodate your veganism?

4. What do you hope to achieve by following a vegan lifestyle?

5. Do you have easy access to vegan food choices daily? YES or NO
   If NO, how do you accommodate the lack of access/availability?

6. Describe the vegan meals and snacks that you eat on a typical day:

7. Do you believe you are adequately nourished from the foods you consume on your vegan meal plan? YES or NO Why or why not?

8. Do you include vegan desserts, snack foods and "fun foods" on a regular basis each week? <u>YES or NO.</u> If not, why?

9. Do you include vegan cheeses on a regular basis each week? <u>YES or NO.</u> If yes, how often? If no, why not?

10. Do you include vegan meats on a regular basis each week? <u>YES or NO.</u> If yes, how often? If no, why not?

11. Do you ever have a craving for non-vegan foods? <u>YES or NO.</u> If yes, what specific non-vegan foods do you crave? How do you respond when you crave a non-vegan food?

12. Do you ever have a craving for specific vegan foods? <u>YES or NO.</u> If yes, what specific vegan foods do you crave?

    How do you respond when you crave a specific vegan food?

13. Do you ever binge on non-vegan foods after previously denying yourself the option to consume it? <u>YES or NO</u> If YES, what are your non-vegan binge-food choices? How do you respond when you binge on non-vegan food(s)?

14. Do you ever binge on vegan foods after previously denying yourself the option to consume more of it? <u>YES or NO</u>   If YES, what are your vegan binge-food choices?

    How do you respond when you binge on vegan food(s)?

15. How do you respond when a non-vegan food that is usually avoided is accidentally encountered and/or eaten?

16. Has the elimination of specific food(s) become part of your identity? <u>YES or NO</u> If YES, in what ways?

17. Based on 0-100%, how much does each of the following reasons support your decision to become vegan?
    - Health   %
    - Weight   %
    - Environment   %
    - Ethics   %

18. Are you willing to increase the **portions** of your vegan meal plan to fully nourish your body and brain as necessary? <u>YES</u>   or NO

19. Are you willing to increase the **variety** of fuel choices in your vegan meal plan to fully nourish your body and brain as necessary? <u>YES</u>   or NO

20. Are you willing to consume **"fun foods"** such as vegan ice cream, vegan chocolates, vegan cookies, or vegan cakes on a regular basis? <u>YES</u>   or NO

21. Are you willing to eat vegetarian foods (w/ eggs, dairy) in a social setting to adequately nourish your body if vegan options are not available? <u>YES</u>   or NO

22.   Are you willing to plan, bring and consume a nutritionally adequate quantity and variety of vegan foods to a social setting if vegan options are not provided? <u>YES</u>   or <u>NO</u>

23.   On a scale of 1 (never) to 10 (always), how motivated are you to explore your patterns of eating to reach true food freedom with the support of your treatment team?

What would need to change to increase your motivation?

Figure 12.1 *Separating My Food Beliefs from My Eating Disorder Questionnaire created by Tammy Beasley, MS, RDN, CEDS-S, LD, and Melainie Rogers, MS, RD, CEDRD-S*

Created by Tammy Beasley, MS, RDN, CEDS-S, LD, and Melainie Rogers, MS, RD, CEDRD-S.

In assessing clients' vegan journeys and motivations, Assistant Professor at the University of Montana's Department of Psychology, Caitlin Martin-Wagar, PhD, makes the following suggestions (C. Martin-Wagar, personal communication, March 7, 2022):

Plan ahead! For people not in recovery, going a few extra hours without food because of a lack of availability won't necessarily impact them psychologically. For vegans recovering from eating disorders, accidental restriction can trigger eating disorder urges like binging, purging, and further restriction. Make sure you always have a backup snack/plan if you are going somewhere that may not have vegan options available to you.

If you notice restriction urges are triggered from not having certain foods that are not included in vegan lifestyles, remind yourself that you are not excluding these foods due to eating disordered reasons. Challenge these thoughts and show yourself you are willing to have high-fat vegan foods at times—this can help squash any concerns that you are restricting for eating disordered reasons.

Often, people choose veganism around the same time they develop their eating disorders (teens or early 20s), making it difficult to determine the source of the veganism. While your veganism may have nothing to do with your eating disorder, because food is involved, it is good to ask yourself important questions to determine why you became a vegan. Make a list with two columns: one with the ethical/moral reasons you are vegan and one with potentially eating disordered reasons you are vegan (if there are any). If you discover there are eating disordered reasons for your veganism, find ways to challenge those reasons and refocus on the ethical reasons you are vegan if you want to maintain a vegan lifestyle. For example, you can make sure you are including a wide variety of foods in your diet, including the vegan versions of typical "fun foods," like macaroni and cheese, pizza, and cupcakes.

Challenge myths related to the body sizes/weights of vegans. Vegans come in all shapes and sizes, just like non-vegans!

Megan Boswell, Accredited Practising Dietitian at Plant Nutrition and Wellness (2022), offers the following:

If you are struggling with eating disorder recovery on a vegan or plant-based diet, here are some questions you can ask yourself to work out whether there is a link between the two:

When did you start following a plant-based diet? Was it before or after developing disordered eating habits?

What was your intention for eating plant-based? Has it changed over time? If it was related to 'clean eating' or attempts to change your body shape or size, this may be a red flag.

Do you eat plant-based 'fun foods' such as chocolate, crisps, cream, pizza, burgers, ice cream or baked goods? If these foods are 'off-limits,' this may be cause for concern.

Do you have any food rules? Examples include avoiding carbo-hydrates or foods in a packet.

Jessica Steinbech, MPH, RDN (2021), offers the following approach:

Consider making a list of your core values. Do those values align with the ethics of veganism? If not, what other reasons might you be attracted to veganism?

Remember that resisting harm to animals as far as possible and practicable for you is veganism.

According to Brown et al. (2019, p. 3), the therapeutic team "should fully explore and understand their patients' veganism on an individual basis." By extension, Kofsky (2020) says, "If you've chosen to adopt veganism, dig deep and think about the motivation for your choice." Kofsky also suggests asking oneself, "As a vegan, would you eat vegan ice cream? Would you eat vegan "meat" or cheese? This can help navigate where the discomfort or potential eating disorder thoughts live."

According to the Clinical Practice Guidelines for the BC [British Columbia] Eating Disorders Continuum of Services (Gellar et al., 2012, p. 34),

> One of the most beneficial aspects of a nutritional assessment is distinguishing between behaviours that are 'eating disorder' driven vs. those that contribute to the patient's well-being, independent of the eating disorder. For example, a vegetarian lifestyle may be chosen because it restricts intake of high calorie foods vs. adherence to ethical or cultural beliefs.

Then a list of questions is proposed to ascertain said distinction:

> Are there any foods that you find more challenging to eat? Have these foods always been challenging? Do you relate these current struggles to your eating disorder? What makes these foods more challenging for you? What qualities make a food more challenging to eat? What do you fear would happen if you were to eat one of these foods?

Additionally, Meg Salvia, MS, RDN, CDCES, CEDRD-S, of Meg Salvia Nutrition, asks her patients the following questions to determine the role that fear, rigidity, and/or restriction may play in dietary omissions:

> What was the reason for starting a vegan diet? Why follow a vegan eating pattern versus a vegetarian diet (where eggs and/or cheese and milk could be included)? When did the vegetarian or vegan eating pattern start, and how does that compare to the timeline of the eating disorder? How does the vegan diet impact the eating disorder? Is the part of you that aligns with the ED happy about the way vegan dietary restrictions limit your choices? Do non-vegan foods play a role in ED behaviors (for example, are they included in

binge episodes)? How is your ability to nourish yourself impacted by choosing vegan foods? What is enjoyable? What thoughts or reactions come up for you if you consider increasing your range of food choices or challenging the vegan diet? (This question can help explore a values-oriented response from a fear-based response.)

(M. Salvia, personal communication, March 28, 2022)

Salvia refers to a handout (Figure 12.2) created by Jessica Setnick (MS, RD, CED-S) on evaluating food exclusions "according to categories of nutrition, relevance, ability, resilience, balance, and result" (2018) as a tool toward fostering effective conversation:

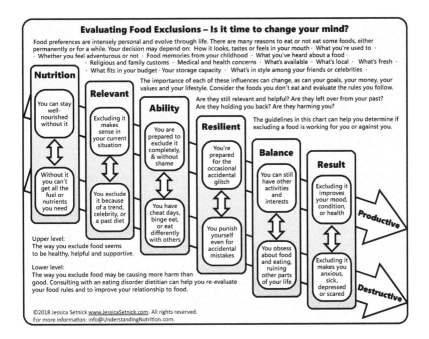

Figure 12.2 *Jessica Setnick's handout for evaluating food exclusions*

The British Dietetic Association's Mental Health group proposes the "key points for an Eating Disorder team to ask to identify if a vegan diet may be related to the development of an eating disorder":

Remember to check if the veganism is part of a religion e.g. Hare Krishna. If a person is following a vegan diet as part of their religion, it is likely to not be associated with their eating disorder. However, it is important to note that most religions endorse 'necessity over prohibition' i.e. people can be exempt from dietary restrictions or fasting for the sake of their physical and mental health.

Does your family follow a vegan diet? What does your family think about your decision to eat a vegan diet?

When did you decide to adopt a vegan diet? If this does not pre-date the onset of the eating disorder and in a context of growing dietary restrictions then this can be considered as a 'red flag' for clinicians.

Was the initial decision to adopt a vegan diet made based on concern for animal welfare or environmental sustainability etc. or was it a health-based decision? If for health concerns or [if] dietary changes were motivated by inappropriate weight loss this can also be considered a 'red flag.'

Is there any 'growing' restriction within the diet? i.e. did this start off as 'healthy eating' then vegetarianism or restrictions of food groups. Are there any self-diagnosed or not medically confirmed restrictions in the diet e.g. lactose free or gluten free?

While acknowledging that following a vegan diet will require a level of nutritional vigilance and checking of ingredients, when looking at foods to identify suitability are there additional nutritional considerations that are in place e.g. avoiding foods with 'red' labels or those with high carbohydrate/fat content?

Are you restricting [your] diet or finding suitable balanced alternatives? Restriction of 'scary' or 'fear' foods and an increase in 'safe' foods.

Do you allow yourself to eat high calorie foods socially? E.g. vegan muffins, brownies, chips, crisps, cheesecake or chocolate cake? Are other people allowed to cook for you? I.e. is the concern about the food being vegan or is it that the illness is trying to control the preparation methods and portions, etc.?

Are ethical choices seen in non-food aspects of life e.g. clothes, toiletries, use of free time?

How are natural errors managed? With an understanding that nobody is 100% perfect or is there a sense of guilt, shame or further exclusion from the diet?

Social effects of eating—can you eat in front of others without knowing the calorie content of the meal/snack, can you eat in front of others, in restaurants etc. . . ?

Social media: is your vegan diet on social media, do you follow fellow vegans and other people with eating disorders? We know that frequent users of multiple social media platforms are more likely to develop a mental health problem (Lin et al., 2016). Note—responsible social media use is appropriate and not linked to disordered eating e.g. following The Vegan Society etc. would be appropriate but not a site that advertises the benefits of dietary restriction (Fuller, 2019, pp. 8–9).

Thoroughly preparing a vegan patient for sustained recovery may entail continual exploration of their unique relationship to veganism. Continual assessments throughout treatment in accordance with the client's physical and psychological progress will help professionals assess both the authenticity and pragmatism of a client's alignment with the dietary component of veganism in both principle and practice (Fuller, 2019; Beasley, 2020). Beasley (2020) states that the questions in the aforementioned "Separating My Food Beliefs from My Eating Disorder" questionnaire "empower clients to begin discovering where the eating disorder beliefs overlap with their vegan beliefs." Furthermore, "as clients retake these assessment questions over the course of treatment and participate in the therapeutic process built on trust in their treatment team, the behaviors that are either separate or enmeshed become more apparent."

Standardized Assessment Considerations

Additionally, it is worth considering psychological test-scoring mechanisms, as certain ones are innately more individualized than others. One way of ensuring heightened accuracy is to distinguish between test objectivity and test subjectivity. Objective tests produce the same scores across test takers for a particular answer regardless of the rater. By contrast, subjective tests can produce different scores on a particular answer "depending on the individual rater" (Hays, 2017, p. 234). Another way of ensuring more accurate individual analysis is to consider whether the assessment is "nomothetic," which uses "common variables that apply to all people," or "idiographic," which uses "unique variables that apply only to the individual" and, as such, "show lawful or meaningful distinctions among people" (pp. 23–24).

Both the Eating Attitudes Test (EAT-26) (Garner et al., 1982) and the Eating Disorder Examination Questionnaire (EDE-Q) (Fairburn & Beglin, 2008) assessments are specific to eating disordered thoughts, feelings, and behaviors (Berg et al., 2011). While there are shortcomings—for example, the EDE-Q has been shown to have lower effectiveness in males (Rose et al., 2013)—overall, they have been accepted as tools for diagnosing eating disorders. The EDE-Q has been validated by, for example, Luce and Crowther (1999); and the EAT-26 has been validated by, for example, Penelo et al. (2013). Also, in some cases, researchers have used the ORTO-11 and ORTO-15 tests when assessing for veganism's inclusion in orthorexia. It is worth noting that the ORTO-11 test is an improved version of the ORTO-15, which, according to Heiss et al., is able to "differentiate between types of meat avoiders, but given the difference in health focus between groups, the scale may be tapping into a construct other than pathological eating beliefs and behaviors" (2019, p. 93). It is also worth investigating how the ORTO-11 has evolved from the ORTO-15 regarding its assessment of such pathology.

I wonder whether, in addition to using tests such as the EAT-26, the EDE-Q, and the ORTO-11, it might be beneficial to consider using the Eating Disorder Inventory 3 (EDI-3) assessment with patients who identify as vegan. The EDI-3 might serve as a tool toward gathering nuanced information and a prompt toward facilitating open-ended therapeutic discussion. The EDI-3 has been regarded as an effective assessment of eating disorders (Friborg et al., 2013). I also wonder about the possible effectiveness of using the General and Eating Disorder Specific Flexibility: Development and Validation of the Eating Disorder Flexibility Index (EDFLIX) Questionnaire, which effectively measures "both general and ED specific cognitive-behavioral flexibility" and, in doing so, accounts for "the conceptual distinction between general and ED related flexibility" (Dahlgren et al., 2019, pp. 1–2). The focus on both types of flexibility may help therapists identify a client's perception of their eating disorder as well as their perception of other aspects of their lives.

Additionally, the "food choice questionnaire" (Steptoe et al., 1995) assesses "dietary restraint and eating style," "value of health," and "social desirability" (p. 271). It identifies "nine distinct factors" (p. 279), which are health, mood, convenience, sensory appeal, natural content, price, weight control, familiarity, and ethical concern. Lindeman and Väänänen (2000) found that this questionnaire's "three new scales, Ecological Welfare (including subscales for Animal Welfare and Environment Protection), Political Values and Religion, [were] reliable and valid instruments for a brief screening of ethical food choice reasons" (p. 55). Therefore, this questionnaire might help contextualize certain concepts, including veganism's equation to restriction.

I also wonder whether looking at specific factors of eating disorder assessments alongside veganism traits would prove effective in assessing a vegan eating disordered patient. For example, expanding on the earlier distinction between eating disorder perfectionism versus vegan perfectionism, it may be worth considering the "perfectionism" aspect of the EDI-3. This perfectionism scale measures both "personal perfectionistic standards" (pressures put upon oneself) and "parental perfectionistic standards" (pressures coming from "parents and teachers") (Garner, 2004). Another potentially overlapping trait among eating disorders and veganism could be the test's category of "personal alienation," which assesses "content reflecting feelings of being separated from, losing out, or not being given due credit from others" (Garner, 2004). However, as discussed in Chapter 7, this variable is also a symptom of "vystopia" (Mann, 2018, p. 38) and ought to be explored as such. "Overcontrol" can become confused with veganism as, according to Garner (2004), "it usually denotes self-defining constructs resistant to change because of their association with virtue." Additionally, the test's measurement of "interpersonal insecurity" accounts for "the tendency to withdrawal and isolate from others" (Garner, 2004). Such insecurity has indeed been experienced in vegans regarding veganism alone, as seen in Chapter 7's discussion of veganism and trauma. "Asceticism" measures "the tendency to seek virtue through the pursuit of spiritual ideals such as self-discipline, self-denial, self-restraint, self-sacrifice and control of bodily urges" (Garner). It includes "the concept that self-denial makes a person stronger" as well as "the tendency to view pleasure, relaxing and human weakness as shameful" (Garner, 2004). When this presentation is conflated with veganism, its presentation may be falsely attributed to vegan-motivated rigidity.

Assessments, like studies, can serve as jumping-off points for more nuanced deliberation. The results of an assessment regarding veganism may help the eating disorder professional better understand the patient and, in doing so, form a holistic picture of what optimal treatment may look like—including the topic of vegan values. The approaches discussed in this chapter may facilitate patients' exploration, reflection, and autonomy. The point is to make the patient feel safe, no matter what that safety looks like and no matter how it may manifest in treatment.

References

Beasley, T. (R. D. N.) (2020, May 15). *Veganism and eating disorder recovery.* Alsana®. Retrieved April 7, 2022, from www.alsana.com/blog/eating-disorder-recovery-bringing-vegans-into-the-fold/

Berg, K. C., Peterson, C. B., Frazier, P., & Crow, S. J. (2011). Psychometric evaluation of the eating disorder examination and eating disorder examination-questionnaire: A systematic review of the literature. *The International Journal of Eating Disorders*, 45(3), 428–438. https://doi.org/10.1002/eat.20931

Boswell, M. (2022, February 28). Eating disorder recovery on a vegan or plant-based diet. *Plant Nutrition & Wellness*. Retrieved April 6, 2022, from www.plantnutritionwellness.com/eating-disorder-recovery-on-a-vegan-or-plant-based-diet/

Brown, A., Fuller, S., & Simic, M. (2019). *Consensus statement on considerations for treating vegan patients with eating disorders.* The Royal College of Psychiatrists, The British Dietetic Association and BEAT. www.rcpsych.ac.uk/docs/default-source/members/faculties/eating-disorders/vegan-patients-eating-disorders-mar19.pdf?sfvrsn=be96d428_2

Dahlgren, C. L., Hage, T. W., Wonderlich, J. A., & Stedal, K. (2019). General and eating disorder specific flexibility: Development and validation of the eating disorder flexibility index (EDFLIX) questionnaire. *Frontiers in Psychology*, 10. https://doi.org/10.3389/fpsyg.2019.00663

Fairburn, C. G., & Beglin, S. (2008). Appendix B: Eating disorder examination questionnaire (EDE-Q6.0). In *Cognitive behavior therapy and eating disorders*. The Guilford Press.

Friborg, O., Clausen, L., & Rosenvinge, J. H. (2013). A five-item screening version of the Eating Disorder Inventory (EDI-3). *Comprehensive Psychiatry*, *54*(8), 1222–1228. https://doi.org/10.1016/j.comppsych.2013.05.004

Fuller, S. (2019). (PDF) *Practice guidance: Veganism and eating disorders*. Retrieved April 8, 2022, from www.researchgate.net/publication/3347 92429_Practice_Guidance_Veganism_and_Eating_Disorders

Garner, D. (2004). *Eating disorder inventory-3 (EDI-3) professional manual*. Psychological Assessment Resources.

Garner, D. M., Olmsted, M. P., Bohr, Y., & Garfinkel, P. E. (1982). The eating attitudes test: Psychometric features and clinical correlates. *Psychological Medicine*, *12*(4), 871–878. https://doi.org/10.1017/s0033291700049163

Geller, J., Goodrich, S., Chan, K., Cockell, S., & Srikameswaran, S. (2012, September 1). Clinical practice guidelines for the British Columbia eating disorder continuum of services. *InsideOut*. https://insideoutinstitute.org.au/resource-library/clinical-practice-guidelines-for-the-british-columbia-eating-disorder-continuum-of-services.

Hays, D. G. (2017). *Assessment in counseling: Procedures and practices*. American Counseling Association.

Heiss, S., Coffino, J. A., & Hormes, J. M. (2019). What does the ORTO-15 measure? Assessing the construct validity of a common orthorexia nervosa questionnaire in a meat avoiding sample. *Appetite*, *135*, 93–99. https://doi.org/10.1016/j.appet.2018.12.042

Kofsky, R. (2020, July 27). *Veganism and eating disorders* (M. S. Mora, Ed.). Integrated Eating. www.integratedeating.com/blog/2020/7/27/veganism-and-eating-disorders.

Lin, L., Sidani, J., Shensa, A., Radovic, A., Miller, E., Colditz, J., Hoffman, B., Giles, L., & Primack, B. (2016). Association between social media use and depression among U.S. young adults. *Depression and Anxiety*, *33*(4), 323–331.

Lindeman, M., & Väänänen, M. (2000). Measurement of ethical food choice motives. *Appetite*, *34*(1), 55–59. https://doi.org/10.1006/appe.1999.0293

Luce, K. H., & Crowther, J. H. (1999, March 19). The reliability of the eating disorder examination-Self-report questionnaire version (EDE-Q). *The*

International Journal of Eating Disorders, 25(3), 349–351. https://doi.
org/10.1002/(sici)1098-108x(199904)25:3<349::aid-eat15>3.0.co;2-m

Mann, C. (2018). *Vystopia: The anguish of being vegan in a non-vegan world.*
Communicate31 Pty Ltd.

Penelo, E., Negrete, A., Portell, M., & Raich, R. M. (2013). Psychometric
properties of the Eating Disorder Examination Questionnaire (EDE-Q)
and norms for rural and urban adolescent males and females in Mexico.
PLoS ONE, 8(12). https://doi.org/10.1371/journal.pone.0083245

Rogers, M. (2019, November 8). *Can you remain vegan & recover from an
eating disorder?* BALANCE Eating Disorder Treatment Center™. Retrieved
April 8, 2022, from https://balancedtx.com/blog/can-you-remain-vegan-
recover-from-an-eating-disorder

Rose, J. S., Vaewsorn, A., Rosselli-Navarra, F., Wilson, G. T., & Weissman,
R. S. (2013). Test-retest reliability of the Eating Disorder Examination-
Questionnaire (EDE-Q) in a college sample. *Journal of Eating Disorders,
1*(1). https://doi.org/10.1186/2050-2974-1-42

Setnick, J. (2018). Handout from eating disorders boot camp: Evaluating
food exclusions. *Understanding Nutrition.* www.understandingnutrition.
com/store/item_view.php?id=1000143&item=handout-from-eating-
disorders-boot-camp%3A-evaluating-food-exclusions.

Steinbech, J. (2021, July 6). *Going vegan in eating disorder recovery.* Taylor
Wolfram. Retrieved April 8, 2022, from www.taylorwolfram.com/vegan-
eating-disorder-recovery/

Steptoe, A., Pollard, T. M., & Wardle, J. (1995). Development of a measure of
the motives underlying the selection of food: The food choice questionnaire. *Appetite, 25*(3), 267–284. https://doi.org/10.1006/appe.1995.0061

13

WORKING WITH AMBIVALENCE AND VALUES

Vegan eating disordered patients may experience eating disordered ambivalence in much the same way that non-vegan eating disordered patients do. However, it is important to note some possible vegan distinctions, especially pertaining to therapeutic interventions that incorporate value identification.

Ego-Syntonic Versus Ego-Dystonic Sense of Self

Let us revisit the "ego-syntonic/dystonic" nature of eating disorders discussed in Chapter 11. As mentioned, a person experiences an ego-syntonic behavior as a part of themself and an ego-dystonic behavior as separate from themself. In that vein, an eating disordered person who restricts and who views their restriction as being in alignment with their eating disorder's priorities may view their restriction as ego-syntonic, while an eating disordered person who binges and who views this bingeing as

DOI: 10.4324/9781003310617-17

being out of alignment with their eating disorder's priorities (in favor of restriction, for example, which they may regard as integral to their eating disordered priorities) may view their bingeing as ego-dystonic. According to Roncero et al. (2014, p. 4),

> In EDs, the identification with the disorder is so marked that patients do not recognize their illness . . . Patients value their attitudes and behaviors as rational, defending them as a way of life that others simply do not understand.

It would therefore make sense that "individuals struggling with disordered eating and related disturbances often have difficulty reporting what they value" (Sandoz et al. 2010, p. 142). A person with an eating disorder is often ambivalent about recovery, but the root of this ambivalence can be difficult to pinpoint. Roncero et al.'s research review found that "the fight against the ambivalence of ED patients is a fight against part of their identities" (2014, p. 9) Subsequently, assessments—and continued treatment—can help in sorting through the person's ambivalence.

Considering Values

Eating disordered individuals may confuse values with unhealthy aims or intentions. On the one hand, they may mistake a value for a "rule about what should or shouldn't be." On the other hand, they may mistake a value for something that aligns with "feeling better" more than it aligns with "doing better" (Sandoz et al., 2010, p. 35). This can be dangerous for the eating disordered person, who may "feel better" due to the perceived relief, comfort, or sense of safety brought about by an eating disorder behavior—the very behavior whose engagement would suggest they are "doing worse."

The benefit of identifying the root of ambivalence is twofold: first, patients may realize that their eating disordered beliefs are essentially not "them" (as opposed to the illusion that the ego-syntonic quality is them and the ego-dystonic quality is not them), and second, they may realize their genuine values.

To the first point: Distinguishing between ego-synotic and ego-dystonic eating disordered behaviors identifies the behaviors the person believes is or is not part of themselves. States that are associated with ego-syntonic behaviors may involve relief, ambition, pride, safety, comfort, familiarity, and/or containment. Ego-syntonic eating disordered behavior seems in line with the eating disorder's agenda and is thus incorporated into the eating disorder's sense of self; it is how it wants to be defined. By contrast, states that are associated with ego-dystonic behaviors may involve shame, fear, anxiety, frustration, and/or guilt. Ego-dystonic eating disordered behaviors seem oppositional to the eating disorder's agenda and thus are cast out. They are not what the eating disordered self wants. They therefore necessitate reprimand.

The eating disordered person, by distinguishing between ego-syntonic and ego-dystonic behaviors, can learn experientially that these behaviors are two sides of the same coin. Both are ultimately negative. Any semblance of the former's supposed positivity is by nature unsustainable and thus fleeting. This perceived positivity is an untrustworthy indicator of the person's actual self-alignment. If the eating disordered person can see these competing states from outside of the eating disordered mindset, they would clearly recognize the disparity and in-fighting. It would be like watching boxers fight with one another in the boxing ring. The eating disordered person, through therapy, may position themselves outside of the arena and look in. Once they do, they can see what is really going on. They can see how the lies perpetuate more lies and how one side's supposed victory is doing nothing more than keeping them both in the ring until neither can see straight.

Through clarifying these ego-syntonic and ego-dystonic distinctions, eating disordered individuals may come to recognize the ongoing loop of internal eating disorder voices fighting and resisting one another. As long as the person's eating disorder voices are fighting one another—as long as those voices continue to take center stage over the person's *actual* voice—the person will be stuck in a loop of alternately failing and appeasing their eating disorder. Recognizing that an internal fight exists grants them an opportunity to realize that neither side is inherently their own; it is all "eating disorder." Eating disorders are manipulative. Rendering these two seemingly opposing sides as equally distorted can help the person overcome the eating disorder's manipulation.

To the second point: Once outside of that boxing ring, the person, while likely disoriented, is positioned to distinguish their own genuine values in contrast to their eating disordered supposed values or priorities. They get to recognize that which actually sustains and compels them. They become lucid; their genuine experience becomes more vivid as they experience themselves as alive rather than at the mercy of perpetual distraction from their aliveness. They get to embody themselves on their own terms. They get to recognize where their own sense of purpose begins and work toward embracing it. This is a process; it will likely not come automatically. It will likely involve retraining the mind and body to adjust to this newfound aliveness. There may be ambivalence in this process. The work it takes to grow from here can feel even harder than the work it took to fight within the eating disorder's grip because there could be a vast unknown territory, with self-doubt and eating disorder triggers left and right. An eating disordered person who begins to recover does not automatically know who they are without their eating disorder. In fact, a new absence of the eating disorder might seem to leave a gap or a feeling of limbo. In this state, it may feel tempting or even necessary to go back to eating disorder behaviors. *At least that world was known to me,* they might think. In my experience, it took work, time, and consistency to get myself back. It was not automatic. It essentially felt like growing myself again from scratch, like reformatting myself to my self. I was living in a foreign world for a good while.

It takes active work for an eating disordered person to grow from this point. A person needs to go out of their way for growth to happen. A person needs to actively create this growth. This is why the thoughtful and thorough assessment of a patient's true versus eating disordered values is essential to their sustained and deepening recovery. Decisions about whether to eat vegan during treatment matter, not only so the patient may eat in accordance with their values, but also so that the patient may feel, connect with, remember, and continually realize who they are versus who their eating disorder had them believing they were. The effects of beneficial assessment thus far transcend the treatment duration; rather, they may set the stage for the person to have a sustainable recovery and a meaningful life in the long-term. The person doing this work in treatment may establish a firmer foundation upon which to position their authentic self. This is the work of continuous living. It is the point at which eating disorder treatment becomes eating disorder recovery. The field would therefore do wonders by these patients to prioritize consideration of their values.

If we approach conversations about recovery through the lens of understanding and respecting a person's vegan values, then a genuine, non-defensive deliberation may evolve wherein the provider is perceived as being in alignment with their patient's truth. One way to enact this alignment is to speak from a perspective of understanding the definition of veganism. Specifically, instead of asking, "What is *impossible* for you?" and lumping veganism into the list of potentially impossible things, a provider might ask, "What is *practicably possible* for you as a vegan?"

For some patients, this treatment may take the form of not eating a completely vegan diet, but rather just doing their best. After all, eating disorder recovery naturally involves conquering all-or-nothing thinking (discussed in Chapter 6), and thus, forgiving oneself for a slip-up is important. A particular patient may have a treatment goal of practicing kindness toward themselves if unable to eat entirely vegan on a particular day. Maybe this person's treatment would involve accepting their need to take time transitioning back to veganism's dietary component. Maybe a vegan patient's goal would be to recognize all the ways in which they *are* living according to their values—are they still abstaining from wearing leather or wool, for example? Fuller (2019, p. 9) suggests that clients whose veganism seems conflated with restriction may consider continuing to practice non-dietary components of veganism throughout treatment, such as "purchasing cruelty free makeup, not purchasing leather goods, purchasing vegan clothes, using vegan laundry powders/ washing up liquids, using environmentally friendly and ethical banks/ energy providers etc."

If we understand that the same mentality would apply to a vegan whose eating disorder recovery would require them—in some alternate universe—to wear fur, maybe we can better understand that what is most important is a value rather than food. We must relate to vegans on the premise that their veganism is a value system. We must meet them there instead of solely focusing on the value system's dietary component, keeping the conversation tethered to a "yes you can, no you can't" narrative or looking at veganism through a solely practical lens. After all, isn't this what therapy is about? Isn't this again the heart and soul of it?

We need to meet the client at the underlying meaning of whatever is showing up on the surface. If we only treat vegan actions, such as not eating or wearing anything derived from animals, then treatment will not deal with the client's true values. The clinician must understand a particular client's values by listening to their client as though they had never heard anyone bring up the subject before. In truth, they have never heard anyone bring it up in a way that this particular client has, even if it has led to the same outcome. Incorporating openness and curiosity into assessments with eating disordered patients—vegan or not—will likely serve them well. In describing his concept of "empathic understanding," Rogers (1961, p. 62) says, "When someone understands how it feels and seems to be *me*, without wanting to analyze me or judge me, then I can blossom and grow in that climate." Everyone in eating disorder treatment benefits from the recognition of their values during treatment. This recognition will be reflected differently in each vegan's individual treatment plan, but one ostensible commonality will be the benefit of working in support of—rather than in resistance to—values that a vegan patient expressively holds.

I will now propose some approaches with which to consider a vegan eating disordered person's ambivalence and values.

Acceptance and Commitment Therapy

Acceptance and commitment therapy (ACT) aims to determine whether a person's values are in line with their behavior. In doing so, it aims to help people make choices that align with their values. As discussed, eating disordered individuals may confuse values for something that makes them feel good (read: makes the eating disorder comfortable) and subsequently avoid action that is difficult (or that does not feel good). As a response, ACT may help an eating disordered person "engage in behavior that is difficult and without immediate consequences because it serves that thing they value" (Sandoz et al., 2010, p. 35). Such work may facilitate a subsequent "shift from a life dominated by aversive control to a life guided by chosen values" (Sandoz et al., 2010, p. 143).

ACT could have specific benefits for ethically vegan eating disordered patients. As discussed in Chapter 6, vegan eating disordered individuals are capable of experiencing freedom in their recovery. Their version of recovery, just like anyone else's, would involve incorporating flexibility. As such, it is worth noting that its goal "for eating disorders is psychological flexibility with the purpose of facilitating valued living" (Sandoz et al., 2010, p. 80). As with many eating disordered individuals, a vegan eating disordered person may have difficulty challenging themselves to eating a wide variety of food. The key, however, is to remember that, for the ethical vegan, this challenge will always fall within the parameters of veganism. So vegan cake could be very scary for a vegan in recovery! It certainly was for me. ACT could help a vegan, like it would anyone else, work toward greater flexibility in their food intake. An ACT approach could help both patients and professionals to genuinely align with a vegan patient's potential for eating disordered freedom.

It is important for the therapeutic alliance (discussed in Chapter 14) to be prioritized early on so that the patient can be as honest as possible with themselves and their therapist about their values. If trust is carefully established, this discussion can be a great jumping-off point from which to explore a patient's vegan motivation. It can prompt further discussion about the extent to which the patient feels that their values align with their vegan behaviors. More detailed questions may follow, and the patient can be gently challenged as the therapist sees fit.

Motivational Interviewing

Therapists and related professionals may draw on elements of motivational interviewing (MI)—a "collaborative, goal-oriented style of communication with particular attention to the language of change"—by guiding patients through their ambivalence and toward an autonomous motivation and subsequent desire to change (Miller & Rollnick, 2013, p. 29). MI's priority of targeting high ambivalence may be significant for vegan eating disordered individuals as a means toward drawing out their true versus false values.

A Combination

Assessing one's own values via ACT and MI techniques may help to identify the person's authentic values versus their disordered or inauthentic values. Using the values component of ACT in combination with motivational interviewing could contribute to a patient's authentic identification of their driving force. Since eating disordered patients are often ambivalent about recovery, drawing from elements of these techniques may help them become clear about why they want to change and what it would take to change. They could become honest with themselves and their therapist about the role that maintaining their vegan diet will play in either helping or hindering them in making this change. After all, if they are able to clarify what it is they want to change and are able to identify a motivation within them to change (as built into the principles of MI), then it would stand to reason that they might choose actions that would help them get there rather than actions that would deter them.

Eating Disorder–Specific Challenges

Do these approaches guarantee an effective outcome for eating disorder clients? Having discussed ambivalence and often compromised physical and mental health, I am inclined to say it is not a guarantee. However, let us consider that motivational interviewing has shown some promise with eating disordered patients (Ziser et al., 2021; Cassin & Geller, 2015, pp. 344–364). Furthermore, let us consider that recovery does not need to be the patient's identified goal in the motivational interviewing process. Finally, let us consider adapting Eugene Gendlin's concept of "life-forward movement" toward formulating a motivational interviewing goal. Perhaps, like Gendlin, a therapist might pose the question, "What might it be that points 'toward more life'?" (1996, Kindle location 3995–3997). This inquiry necessitates the therapist's "value neutrality" unless they "take a stand in favor of a client's life-forward direction." However, much like motivational interviewing principles, "the ultimate criterion is the client's own further experiencing and differentiating" (Gendlin, 1996, Kindle location 4087–4091).

Vegan-Specific Value Considerations

Getting to the heart of a vegan patient's values could involve recognizing how their feelings motivate them. Therapists may inquire how patients' feelings might be channeled toward their values in purposeful ways. A therapist may support a vegan in better understanding how their values may align with their sense of purpose as a vegan.

I have discussed the importance of identifying a vegan eating disordered person's relationship to their eating disordered trajectory, what drives their eating disorder forward, what that supposed eating disordered sense of purpose really means. Now, we might also ask: How does the vegan person connect to their vegan trajectory? How do vegan eating disordered individuals relate to various vegan-specific processes and outcomes? What drives this vegan eating disordered individual's veganism forward? How does this vegan eating disordered individual enact their vegan-related purpose in the world?

This support might incorporate a discussion of deontological versus consequentialist vegan orientations. A study by Judge et al., on "what motivates individuals to promote, or encourage others to adopt, a vegan lifestyle" (2021, p. 1) found that "the frequency of engaging in vegan activism is predicted by similar variables to those that predict collective action in other identity-based contexts (e.g., collective action surrounding racial justice or environmental justice)" (p. 2). Knowing this may make it easier for a professional to conceptualize veganism as a social movement rather than a diet.

The drive toward life makes the eating disorder less powerful, as the client can clearly see how it is sabotaging that goal. The extent to which the client falls back into the eating disorder may be the extent to which they distance themselves from the other, life-forward goal. But I have two points to add to this prospect. First, the person is now engaged in a tug-of-war instead of a one-directional pull, so the very process of the assessment is therapeutically beneficial. Second, this type of therapeutic approach would ideally happen at multiple points throughout treatment, such that the person will—with proper nourishment, curbing of eating disorder behaviors, continued therapy, and interpersonal practice—be increasingly likely to benefit from their engagement with it. With that, they may be better positioned to authentically identify both their goal and the steps they believe will get them there. As they progress through treatment, they will be increasingly able to navigate the ambivalence that motivational interviewing is designed to address.

Person-Centered Reflecting of Ego-Syntonic Congruence and Ego-Dystonic Incongruence

According to Aspen et al. (2014, p. 1), "Individuals with eating disorders who experience their behaviors as congruent with their personality and have a certain amount of pride in the ability to diet and exercise to extremes view the eating disorder as ego-syntonic. In most cases, when the eating disorder is experienced as ego-syntonic, there will be little or no motivation to change the behaviors." Aspen et al.'s statements speak to the earlier point about the importance of identifying ego-syntonic versus ego-dystonic behaviors. Similarly, the ego-syntonic congruence (and, by contrast, the ego-dystonic incongruence) to which the authors refer may be viewed in parallel to Rogers's principles of congruence (alignment of awareness and experience) versus incongruence (misalignment of awareness and experience). Notably, since incongruence's "state is one of tension and internal confusion" (1959, p. 203), and since eating disordered individuals often struggle with ambivalence, a therapist of an eating disordered client may mirror the client's increasing determination as it happens, showing the client that recognizing their own authenticity is possible—after all, the therapist is recognizing their own authenticity by authentically reacting to that of the client.

References

Aspen, V., Darcy, A. M., & Lock, J. L. (2014). Patient resistance in eating disorders. *Psychiatric Times*. Retrieved April 7, 2022, from www.psychiatrictimes.com/view/patient-resistance-eating-disorders

Cassin, S. E., & Geller, J. (2015). Motivational interviewing in the treatment of disordered eating. In H. Arkowitz, W. R. Miller, & S. Rollnick (Eds.), *Motivational interviewing in the treatment of psychological problems* (pp. 344–364). The Guilford Press.

Fuller, S. (2019). (PDF) *Practice guidance: Veganism and eating disorders*. Retrieved April 8, 2022, from www.researchgate.net/publication/334792429_Practice_Guidance_Veganism_and_Eating_Disorders

Gendlin, E. T. (1996). *Focusing-oriented psychotherapy a manual of the experiential method*. The Guilford Press.

Judge, M., Fernando, J. W., & Begeny, C. T. (2022). Dietary behaviour as a form of collective action: A social identity model of vegan activism. *Appetite*, *168*, 105730. https://doi.org/10.1016/j.appet.2021.105730

Miller, W. R., & Rollnick, S. (2013). *Motivational interviewing: Helping people change* (3rd ed.). The Guilford Press.

Rogers, C. R. (1959). A theory of therapy, personality, and interpersonal relationships, as developed in the client-centered framework. In S. Koch (Ed.), *Psychology: A study of a science* (Vol. 3, pp. 184–256). McGraw-Hill.

Rogers, C. R. (1961). *On becoming a person: A therapist's view on psychotherapy*. Houghton Mifflin.

Roncero, M., Belloch, A. B., & Perpiñá, C. (2014). Ego-Syntonicity and eating disorders. In C. Gramaglia & P. Zeppegno (Eds.), *New developments in anorexia nervosa research*. Nova Biomedical.

Sandoz, E. K., Wilson, K. G., & DuFrene, T. (2010). *Acceptance and commitment therapy for eating disorders: A process-focused guide to treating anorexia and bulimia*. New Harbinger Publications.

Ziser, K., Rheindorf, N., Keifenheim, K., Becker, S., Resmark, G., Giel, K. E., Skoda, E.-M., Teufel, M., Zipfel, S., & Junne, F. (2021). Motivation-enhancing psychotherapy for inpatients with anorexia nervosa (manna): A randomized controlled pilot study. *Frontiers in Psychiatry, 12.* https://doi.org/10.3389/fpsyt.2021.632660

14

THE THERAPEUTIC ALLIANCE

I believe that the most important part of any client's therapy is the therapeutic relationship. In order to co-create a meaningful therapeutic relationship, a "therapeutic alliance," which is "the trust between patient and therapist that allows them to work together effectively," must be present (Cabaniss et al., 2017). In fact, Cabaniss et al. suggested that this alliance "might be the most important part of treatment" (p. 85). In Eugene Gendlin's discussion of "therapeutic avenues"—which he posited to be more flexible than therapeutic modalities—Gendlin referred to "interpersonal interaction" as "the most important therapeutic avenue," since "its quality affects all the other avenues" (1996, Kindle location 4448–4452). Additionally, Carl Rogers (1946, p. 419) put forth that communication was an important component of the therapeutic relationship, such that "if the client feels that . . . his communication is understood rather than evaluated in any way, then he is free to communicate more deeply." According to Rogers, the therapist's main purpose ought to be "providing deep understanding and

DOI: 10.4324/9781003310617-18

acceptance of the attitudes consciously held at this moment by the client as he explores step by step into the dangerous areas which he has been denying to consciousness." (1946, p. 421).

The therapeutic relationship cannot be replicated by any other because every client is unique. According to Wosket, because the relationship is new, it "is not in itself contaminated by old patterns, grudges, betrayals, unfinished business, loss of hope or fixed stances. This makes it fertile and virgin territory for whatever the client needs to plant in it" (1999, location 829). Therefore, the dynamic between the therapist and client is never identical from one client to the next. The same technique will never play out identically between multiple clients because the client is the ever-changing part of the therapist–client pair. The therapist therefore must be both grounded in who they are and adaptable to who their client needs them to be.

A patient's trusted revelation of authentic values depends on the formation and sustainment of a therapeutic alliance. The alliance should be fostered to the best of the professional's ability with regard to the aforementioned principles and approaches. There are many modalities from which therapists can draw while working with eating disorder patients, but the optimal modality still needs to be chosen with the patient's specific needs in mind—needs that can make themselves known in a strengthening therapeutic alliance. Ultimately, no matter which modality the therapist uses, its effectiveness will depend on the quality of the client–therapist relationship. Gendlin says, "All orientations and procedures interfere with psychotherapy insofar as they are held to tightly. Priority must always be given to the person and to the therapist's ongoing connection with the person" (1996, Kindle locations 2274–2277). Likewise, Wosket speaks to the importance of prioritizing the therapist's use of self over a counseling theory. "The self," she says, "is almost infinitely adaptable in having the ability to respond differentially to individual clients and a variety of therapeutic challenges" (1999, Kindle location 744). Regardless of the specific approach or technique a professional employs, I believe that the therapeutic relationship is ultimately at the heart of therapeutic effectiveness.

Eating Disorders and the Therapeutic Alliance

Eating disorder clients are in a specific type of therapeutic setting, of course, involving physical, physiological, and psychological recovery, so I understand there are additional factors when considering their treatment. It is not simply a matter of applying therapeutic tools that may work for someone who has a healthfully nourished brain and body and whose cognitive distortions may directly connect to their compromised physical health.

When working with eating disordered patients, the physiologically compromising nature of the disorder can impact the formation of that alliance. In their meta-analyses on the relationship between eating disorder symptoms and the therapeutic alliance, Graves et al. (2017) found that symptom relief predominantly preceded a strengthened alliance. However, the reverse also held true, albeit in fewer cases. It makes sense that symptom relief would set the stage for an improved alliance. The eating disordered individual may be better able to connect with a therapist once sufficiently and sustainably nourished, even if eating disorder thoughts subsist. It makes sense that a strong alliance at the beginning of treatment would establish the basis for an eating disordered individual to trust someone other than their eating disorder voice.

No matter the order, I hold that forming the therapeutic alliance should be a foundational aspect of a client's treatment. I say this because even if the individual cannot think clearly enough for the alliance itself to prompt a change in symptoms, this early alliance offers a sense of continuity in the therapeutic relationship. The client may associate a later improvement in symptoms with the therapist's consistent, non-judgmental witnessing of them. The client will have a reference point to a more confusing time when someone was trying to reach them—even if at the time, they could not meet the therapist there.

It is important that this alliance is given equal priority to the physical components of recovery. That is to say: the patient can experience the therapist who encouraged them to refrain from engaging in eating disordered behaviors as being the same therapist who saw the best in them before they could see it in themselves. The vegan eating disordered client will be able to say later that their therapist cared about them and not just their symptoms and, as such, recognized their personhood underneath the eating disorder's hold. The vegan person who doesn't eat vegan in treatment can still feel unconditionally regarded by the therapist who never judged any part of them and, in keeping with this initial behavior, continues to not judge them now.

Forming an early alliance with an eating disorder patient is important because once the therapist appears, the patient is no longer alone with their eating disorder. Whether or not they want or accept help, the fact is that their reality has changed: they are now in a position to be helped. This realization might be the scariest thing imaginable for them, but that fear speaks to the fact that this has registered; that "scary recovery," the thing they fear, is, in fact, accessible; that the eating disorder is not the only voice; that "something" is now competing with that voice. Again, it may be the opposite of pleasant, but its presence at the very least cannot be denied. The therapist in this dynamic has a responsibility to consciously cultivate security from the humble beginning.

Vegan Eating Disordered Patients and the Therapeutic Alliance

The client's first impression of the therapist's response to their vegan beliefs affects the client's treatment trajectory. If the client feels like the therapist accepts the ethical basis of their veganism and wants to know more, a strong alliance is being set up. Setting up this strong alliance will lay a foundation for the ongoing sharing of any alternative or additional truths about the client's relationship to veganism. But if therapists don't start with a shared view of the client's outlook, if therapists don't initially align with who the client says they are and what the client says they value, then they risk compromising the client's confidence in their ability to hold space for them later. Without an early focus on establishing alliance, therapists may not be best able to help clients in the way they need; that is to say, in spite of pure intentions, the support may not be as impactful as a therapist would like it to be.

Professionals need not master an understanding about their client's experience with veganism in order to establish congruence in the professional–client relationship. Furthermore, the therapist of a vegan eating disordered client need not know everything in order to believe their client in that moment.

Professionals may feel that voicing their curiosity may impede their attempts to authentically validate their client's reality. However, when authenticity is focused on the relationship first, then the relationship will take precedence over the therapist's ability to fully understand the patient. In this way, a therapist need not fully understand or agree with a client in order to provide authentic therapy. They may even use these differences for the purposes of therapy itself. Additionally, it can be okay to ask questions, so long as they are asked with the sole intent of getting to know the client. Forming a rapport with a vegan client may simply involve a willingness to acquire knowledge about an unfamiliar topic. April Lang, LCSW, SEP, posits that "when working with vegan clients, a little knowledge about veganism and some forethought into potentially sensitive topics/reactions can ensure we're attuned and accessible to these individuals" (A. Lang, personal communication, January 27, 2021).

If a therapist would like a patient to foster reliance on their own strengths, then it is important that the therapist believes that the patient has these resources and is capable of acting on them. The therapist themselves might not choose what the vegan chooses and might not understand how this choice could apply to themselves, but they must nonetheless make space for the reality as it applies to the patient. Indeed, anti-speciesism educator Dallas Rising says,

> I know for a fact that a carnist can help a vegan heal from an eating disorder because I had carnists and vegetarians on my team. If they approach the treatment plan from a place of compassion and centering the needs of the vegan with the eating disorder, they don't have to hold the same values.
> (D. Rising, personal communication, March 24, 2022)

Effective client–therapist collaboration connotes the opposite of collusion. In the case of a vegan client, such collaboration does not have to mean that the therapist agrees with the client's values or agrees with the client about eating vegan in treatment. The therapeutic principles can still be fully and uncompromisingly present while assessing and addressing the physiological components of recovery. This is because wholeness does not imply an inability to be flexible. In fact, if something is complete, dignified, grounded in itself, and unmoved by attempts to make it anything other than what it essentially is, then it can adapt while still being itself. So therapeutic principles may remain intact even when the whole of recovery entails more elements. The therapist holds a level ground with a client swept up in uncertainty, and they collaborate with fellow treatment team members as they work toward whatever the client needs.

References

Cabaniss, D. L., Cherry, S., Douglas, C. J., & Schwartz, A. R. (2017). *Psychodynamic psychotherapy: A clinical manual*. Wiley Blackwell.

Gendlin, E. T. (1996). *Focusing-oriented psychotherapy a manual of the experiential method*. The Guilford Press.

Graves, T. A., Tabri, N., Thompson-Brenner, H., Franko, D. L., Eddy, K. T., Bourion-Bedes, S., Brown, A., Constantino, M. J., Flückiger, C., Forsberg, S., Isserlin, L., Couturier, J., Paulson Karlsson, G., Mander, J., Teufel, M., Mitchell, J. E., Crosby, R. D., Prestano, C., Satir, D. A., Simpson, S., . . . Thomas, J. J. (2017). A meta-analysis of the relation between therapeutic alliance and treatment outcome in eating disorders. *The International Journal of Eating Disorders*, *50*(4), 323–340. https://doi.org/10.1002/eat.22672

Rogers, C. R. (1946). Significant aspects of client-centered therapy. *American Psychologist*, *1*(10), 415–422. https://doi.org/10.1037/h0060866

Wosket, V. (1999). *The therapeutic use of self: Counselling practice, research and supervision*. Routledge.

15

CO-CONSTRUCTING A BROADER WAY FORWARD

The values discussed in preceding chapters are, in one sense, about eating disorders and veganism and in a broader sense, about beneficial client care. If all treatment centers earnestly do their best for their vegan clients, then vegans with eating disorders would have a much greater chance of benefitting from treatment. This is because vegans for whom the only barrier to treatment was being made to eat non-vegan food would likely be more inclined to choose a vegan-accommodating treatment center. There would be a possible light at the end of the eating disorder's tunnel, a possible way out.

Eating disorder treatment in its current form cannot fully accommodate veganism because it is looking at veganism through the lens of a non-vegan treatment norm. Treatment has been built on a model that reflects societal norms that involve eating animals, so the treatment norm is to eat animals. The non-vegan patients in treatment represent the status quo, to which veganism is the alternative. At present, vegan-accommodating

DOI: 10.4324/9781003310617-19

treatment is like trying to fit a square into a circle. By extension, Beasley believes that treatment should "treat" rather than simply "accommodate" vegans (T. Beasley, personal communication, March 23, 2022). Treatment for vegans is often accommodated, seen as going out of one's way, and seen as an exception.

The treatment milieu is a microcosm of society. Although veganism is more mainstream than it has ever been, society is not there yet. This current situation is naturally reflected in treatment; why wouldn't it be? Nothing will change because there is no perceived impetus to change. There is little perceived need to change treatment because it is largely working at the moment—for omnivores.

Interestingly, we normalize the idea that the eating disordered patient has to change—after all, they are in treatment to get better, which necessitates change. However, when considering ethical veganism, it is the field that has to change, not the eating disordered person. The onus should not be on this vegan eating disordered person to change; it should be on the professionals involved in their care. By extension, the onus should be on the larger field to enact change on a more systematic level (see Chapter 18 on a vegan-informed model). The vegan patient should not be responsible for managing the field's shortcomings.

In my opinion, this situation implies that those of us in the position to take in and share information about eating disorders and veganism have to:

- Be patient, acknowledge where we are, and accept imperfection while opening ourselves up to new approaches, all the while recognizing that change will take time and happen incrementally, as long as we head in the right direction. While we are where we are, we have to, at the very least, understand the need to understand. Openness, patience, and understanding, when practiced together, will go a long way toward helping a vegan patient feel supported.
- Go out of our way to make a change. We have to proactively make change happen.

The following are questions that treatment providers might pose when considering how treatment may best support vegan patients. I am specifically addressing treatment providers because they are frequently the recipients, conveyors, and discriminators of information:

- What steps can be taken toward implementing changes in attitudes?
- Short of changing the structure of treatment from the ground up, what can be done with what already exists?
- How can a treatment center do its very best to meet their vegan patients—alongside omnivore patients—where they are?

Change can mean any number of things for an eating disorder treatment center. The solution may not be one hundred percent vegan allowance at every meal but rather that the vast majority of the vegan patients' meals are vegan. It may involve creating a vegan support group within treatment if more than one patient is vegan. It may involve referring a patient to a similar support group off site which they can attend during or after their treatment. It may involve having a discussion with the whole group and encouraging honest and direct communication if there are any misunderstandings.

Perhaps a vegan patient may be permitted to opt out of a non-vegan-accommodating restaurant outing without the added worry that providers will regard them as treatment non-compliant. In such a case, a treatment center may consider implementing an equally challenging situation either on or off site for the vegan patient. For example, in my treatment, individual patients occasionally had the opportunity to go out to restaurants with a staff member. In doing this, I was able to select restaurants with vegan choices.

It is important to acknowledge that vegans in vegan-accommodating treatment centers are reliably participating in restaurant outings and cooking groups. According to Tammy Beasley, MS, RDN, CEDS-S, LD, vegan clients at Alsana "participate in restaurant outings with the entire milieu/community" at "restaurants that can accommodate vegan modifications." Additionally, vegan clients participating in a "'client creation' meal challenge" create vegan meals for "all clients in the milieu," while non-vegan clients "plan for vegan modifications if a vegan client is in the milieu" (T. Beasley, personal communication, August 28, 2020).

In cooking groups, some ingredients may be replaced with vegan versions, and if the meal cannot be made vegan, the patient may opt out of the group. We should recognize that cooking animals and their by-products might be psychologically disturbing for a vegan, and the safer option may actually be non-participation.

Acquiring Knowledge

Adapting to the needs of vegans may garner beneficial results. Pragmatic concerns such as funding and resourcefulness can pose valid obstacles toward delivering ideal care to a vegan patient. However, targeting the obstacle itself may be an act of futility. Besides, even if an obstacle is directly targeted, it will take time to change—time that the patient cannot afford to lose and time that a provider does not necessarily have when trying to be available to all of their patients.

Providers need not fix all obstacles in their purview before addressing treatment of vegan patients. Instead, providers may consider becoming curious about their vegan clients, and they may use this curiosity to identify and subsequently adapt resources toward best serving clients' individual needs. From this curious mindset, professionals may ask: What is the best that can be done given this unfortunate—and perhaps even fixed—obstacle? What can be done?

Whatever steps are taken to improve the quality of eating disorder treatment for vegans, these steps will be effective if they are founded on an increased knowledge of veganism. In building this knowledge of veganism and treatment approaches, let us consider the approaches mentioned throughout this book—particularly in this and the following chapter—as models. How might those models be adapted to specific circumstances?

A treatment center need not have mastered a knowledge of veganism in order to improve its treatment of vegan patients. As discussed in Chapter 6, perfection for a vegan is not the goal; imperfection is inherently understood. Vegans aim to avoid contributing to the exploitation of animals as much as is practicably possible. Therefore, vegans will feel more supported if treatment centers also do as much as is practicably possible.

Like veganism, the construct of treatment is based on an ethical value system: the belief that eating disordered individuals can get better and so should be given the best chance at recovery. Professionals respond to problems that can't be solved on their own—eating disorders. Speaking on behalf of eating disorder sufferers whose eating disorder provided no fundamental impetus to change, therapists may state: *This is going on, and this is what we can do about it.* Nothing will change if nobody does anything to declare that a change is needed. Treatment will still respond to the problem of eating disorders because clients will not spontaneously get better on their own, and treatment will adapt to the needs of eating disordered individuals. Therefore, once the eating disorder field has new knowledge about veganism, it is positioned to do what it has always done—what it was built to do: namely, adapt to its newly acquired knowledge of vegan eating disordered individuals' plights.

Anti-speciesism educator Dallas Rising, who attended the Emily Program on an outpatient individual basis due to a lack of vegan options in its Intensive Outpatient Program (IOP), commends the treatment program's upgraded efforts to make vegan eating accessible for current and future patients. Rising says,

> Veganism is more about what I stand for than what I don't eat. And luckily, The Emily Program's intake team could see that and honored it. At the time, there was no IOP option for vegan meals, but my team did the best that they could to meet my needs in other ways and I relied heavily on the open friends and family support group for a while. I am really happy to know that vegan meals are now offered in the IOP program. The Emily Program deserves enthusiastic applause for being a leader in this regard.
>
> (Rising, 2014)

Rising's statement speaks to the importance of drawing from one's own resources to continually progress. In this way, doing the best you can with what you have can look like "meeting [patients'] needs in other ways" (Rising, 2014), just as it can look like fully accommodating vegan patients. If the actions taken are rooted in wanting the best for vegan patients, then centers that can currently only "meet [patients'] needs in other ways" are optimally situated to progress toward meeting their patients' needs in more ideal ways. The idea is to explore all potential avenues toward supporting vegan patients and remain open to the forming of new avenues.

Following is an example of doing one's best with the resources available despite limitations: Fuller et al.'s study on UK eating disorder specialists found that vegan options for "compulsory nasogastric feeding or treatment with non-vegan medication" was limited. The authors therefore concluded that:

> at present, and in the absence of equivalent vegan enteral feeds and medicines, the best that can be done is to treat the patient as you would any other, while being as collaborative as possible and minimising the use of non-vegan options.
>
> (Fuller et al., 2021, p. 119)

Fuller et al.'s recommendation is in line with the vegan principle of doing "as much as is practicably possible" (The Vegan Society).

If vegans are not being considered valid in their own regard, then they are being regarded by deduction. Treatment, in this case, would consider them by way of what *does not* occur rather than what *may* occur, by that which *standard* recovery *is not* rather than what *vegan* recovery *is*. If this is the primary way of viewing vegans with eating disorders, then the eating disorder field has effectively laid the groundwork for veganism to conflict with recovery. It is possible that the very fabric of treatment, therefore, omits ethical veganism from its protocol.

Much of the work is found in letting oneself feel unsettled with the way things are. After all, if we aren't resisting anything, why change? Allowing something to come into our awareness that prompts our resistance offers an opportunity to evolve. This element of resistance cues us to consider something new. It shines a light on what may not be working and why we may not be okay with that.

Once something is in our awareness, we have more agency in addressing it. This shift in mindset can set the stage for potential options to reveal themselves later. So let us recognize the power contained within becoming aware of something that we were not aware of before. This is a powerfully liberating shift. It is, in fact, the only place from which change can happen. Moreover, failure to acknowledge it poses a potential for risk that—due to lack of awareness—may not be recognized as risk. So now that we've brought this new information into our awareness, how can we apply it to practice? What can we do, within our wheelhouse, to show up for our patients?

References

Fuller, S., Brown, A., Rowley, J., & Elliott-Archer, J. (2021). Veganism and eating disorders: Assessment and management considerations. *BJPsych Bulletin*, *46*(2), 116–120. https://doi.org/10.1192/bjb.2021.37

Rising, D. (2014, December 11). Vegan and in recovery. *The Emily Program*. www.emilyprogram.com/blog/vegan-and-in-recovery/

The Vegan Society. *Definition of veganism*. www.vegansociety.com/go-vegan/definition-veganism

16

PROFESSIONAL COMMUNICATION THROUGHOUT DIFFERENT LEVELS OF CARE

In this chapter, I will provide an overview of the different levels of care (often termed "LoC") in treatment. I will discuss the importance of establishing and maintaining continuity of care both within and across treatment levels. I will consider how an eating disorder patient's veganism may factor into each level of care.

This book focuses, most generally, on the topic of eating disorders and veganism. More specifically, it focuses on eating disorder recovery and veganism. And even more specifically, it focuses on eating disorder treatment and veganism. Within that treatment exists different levels of care, ranging from the most contained setting, e.g., an inpatient unit, to the most autonomous setting, e.g., a weekly outpatient individual therapy session. In between these two ends of the spectrum are multiple levels of care. For the purposes of this chapter, I will discuss three basic levels

DOI: 10.4324/9781003310617-20

of care: individual outpatient treatment, intensive outpatient treatment, (often called "partial hospitalization"), and inpatient treatment.

I recognize that there are other levels of care, variations on the levels of care I mention, and, in general, treatment approaches that fall outside of these categories completely. I acknowledge the significance of these additional approaches. Different types of complementary treatments may be recommended. I hope that what I say here can be adapted to differing approaches as needed. Furthermore, each level of care I discuss may involve couple's/family sessions, family-focused treatment, complementary and/or holistic techniques, and group therapy.[1]

There is also frequent crossover between each level of care. A patient may be transitioning up to a more intensive level of care or down to a less intensive level of care. Professionals operating on an outpatient and/or inpatient basis may include therapists (clinical social workers, clinical mental health counselors, psychologists, etc.), dietitians, general practitioners, nurses and nursing staff, psychiatrists, and social workers specifically in charge of practical matters for the patient (e.g., communicating with insurance companies so the patient can still qualify for treatment, facilitating aftercare plans, etc.). There is a need for communication between treatment providers both across and within a level of care. It is therefore imperative that an eating disorder patient's veganism is met with the same level of integrity at all levels of care and at all times. I will say again that this applies not only to those who are maintaining the dietary component of veganism in their recovery but also for patients whose treatment plans entail non-vegan food for any reason and to patients who, in the future, may realize that their veganism was a guise for their eating disorder.

Individual Outpatient Treatment

Individual outpatient treatment may occur before, after, or in the absence of more intensive treatment. The patient may be seeing a therapist regularly, but they also may be seeing other treatment professionals, e.g., a dietitian,

---

1 In general, group therapy would be supplemental to individual outpatient treatment and integral to intensive outpatient and inpatient treatment.

regularly as well. The individual therapist is situated to assess the patient's current and past eating disorder history and to communicate with other current providers if there is a need to do so. They are also situated to connect with previous providers at the higher levels of care, whether that means connecting with staff from the patient's team in a day-treatment program from which the patient stepped down, or staff at an inpatient facility where the patient is preparing to go. Unlike day-treatment or inpatient teams, the various staff members involved in an individual's weekly outpatient care may be scattered but can still connect with one another. If the client is preparing to transition to more intensive treatment, it is important that the therapist is clear with the other providers about what the client has communicated to them so that this information can be accurately relayed to a supervisor and other members of an upcoming treatment team.

When a patient is in outpatient individual therapy, with or without related treatment providers, and the therapist has assessed that this is the highest level of care that they need, there is plenty of room for autonomy and flexibility as they go about their lives outside of sessions. Perhaps the therapist and patient will come up with some challenging meal ideas and the patient will practice these ideas throughout the week, reporting back to the therapist about how the challenges went. Perhaps built into these challenges will be mindfulness exercises, journaling assignments, or anything that may help the patient process the feeling they may experience before, during, and after they eat a challenging food. The idea would be to therapeutically work through various facets of the patient's life and consider their personal history and future goals. Food is merely one of the facets of this person's life, but it is an obstructing one that is potentially blocking the patient from being where they would like to be.

Intensive Outpatient Treatment

In an intensive outpatient treatment—or partial hospitalization—program, collaboration and structure are intensified for the patient. The patient goes to a program on certain days of the week for a certain amount of time. The time they spend at the program typically involves eating meals with a group of patients and attending group therapy. Each patient typically receives individual therapy as well, but sometimes, patients already see individual therapists outside of the program. So the level of collaboration and a sense of unity may slightly differ depending on the source of a patient's individual therapy. This level of treatment may provide patients unified or varied meals. If the patient has a choice in what to order from a takeout service, they are required to choose a meal that meets nutritional standards set by the facility's dietitian and in accordance with their specific treatment needs. When an outpatient setting does not accommodate vegans, this presents limitations similar to those of inpatient therapy. The vegan person can, of course, on their own accord, eat vegan outside of the treatment center, but this can do little to nullify any negative impact of having to eat non-vegan food while in the center. Regardless of a particular center's protocol, collaboration is imperative. Communicating with a patient's former treatment providers can elicit a shared understanding of the patient's needs. Continuity of care will help toward building a holistic understanding of the patient as well as facilitate a provider's increased capacity to align with the patient's values, needs, and personhood.

Inpatient Treatment

Inpatient care is the highest level of treatment. Patients in inpatient care have likely been impacted by their eating disorder to a severely compromising degree. In inpatient settings, patients frequently take part in individual and group therapy. While the eating disorder voice is probably louder than their own much of the time, this isn't to say that the patient is wholly lost or that they have entirely forgotten themselves. They may, to varying degrees, have forgotten (or hadn't known of) their capacity to recover, live a full life, or experience self-worth. They may feel extremely conflicted—after all, the eating disordered part of them probably didn't want to go into treatment, but another part of them got themselves to treatment. And if their admission was due to some other means, they still arrived. Finding oneself in treatment in spite of oneself is just another manifestation of getting oneself to treatment in spite of one's eating disorder. There is a certain level of surrender that must happen either way for treatment to be effective.

Communication

Importantly, if there was a provider who worked with a patient previously, it may be worth speaking with that provider about how they perceived the patient's veganism. This circles back to the need for individual outpatient therapists to listen and place value on continuity of care—because they are acquiring the knowledge that they may need to communicate to a provider at a higher level of care in the future. And by the time a patient needs a high level of care they are in such a vulnerable position, it is of the utmost importance that this communication is carried out with the patient's dignified personhood at the forefront of the therapist's mind. Just the same, a therapist in an inpatient setting is responsible for communicating their takeaway from the patient to the other members of the patient's inpatient team. Hence, it is essential for the patient to be heard.

Communication and collaboration across and between all levels of care is imperative to a patient's recovery. A vegan patient whose ethics are based in vegan values deserves to be heard, acknowledged, and supported as much as possible in any treatment setting. Treatment providers should use assessments openly and curiously. Providers should continually assess throughout treatment. Providers should consider how off-site meal and weekend passes worked. Did the patient eat vegan meals outside of the unit, and how did they feel? How did it go? Did they challenge their eating disorders in the process of choosing, eating, and digesting their meal? Did they socialize at all if they tend to isolate? Or did they purposefully eat alone if they tend to be around people in order to avoid eating or distract themselves from connecting with their food? Providers should see where a patient's mindset and clarity of thought and belief about themselves and their disorder and general cognitive distortions are at the beginning of treatment and at different points throughout their treatment. Also, they should consider where the patient is as they near the end of their treatment and prepare for stepping down to less intensive treatment, using the knowledge obtained from a place of authenticity, flexibility, and collaboration throughout their care. The aim should be to set up the strongest foundation possible for the patient to continue to explore, experience, collaborate, change their mind, and live their life on their own terms versus their eating disorder's terms, as they transition to a less intensive level of care that offers them greater autonomy and flexibility as they go about their days.

The nature of an eating disorder is such that it is unstable. The eating disordered patient's world is not secure. Rather, it is chaotic and often frightening. There is a part of the person who knows themselves and a part of the person who feels estranged from themselves. Treatment needs to provide a sense of security throughout the process of recovery. Treatment needs to be the one part of recovery that can withstand chaos. This means showing up for and with the patient in a unified front as treatment collaborators. It doesn't necessitate that all treatment providers agree with each other, but it does necessitate an ability to navigate disagreement as a team. No matter the level of care, it is both possible and necessary to help the patient feel anchored to their treatment team. If the treatment foundations are strong, the patient is anchored in the prospect of recovery at all times, no matter how far from it they may stray.

17

PROFESSIONAL SELF-REFLECTIVE PRACTICE

Professionals in the eating disorder field may perceive veganism in a negative light without realizing they are doing so. If a negative bias toward veganism goes unrecognized, the professional's treatment of vegan patients may pose a detriment to recovery. As veganism can be a highly charged, emotionally laden topic, its discourse can be fraught with judgment from all angles— so much so that both vegans and non-vegans may enact defenses in both professional and non-professional settings. This is an entirely natural— even conditioned—response, one that professionals are not exempt from experiencing unless they have developed an acute understanding of their own stances (in addition to any history surrounding these stances prior to entering a discussion).

Considering the extent to which negative perceptions of veganism and eating disorders exist in the eating disorder field, it is fair to surmise the field's general mistrust of veganism's presence in the eating disordered person's life. Professionals are vulnerable to lacking clinical neutrality

DOI: 10.4324/9781003310617-21

when working with vegan patients because an assessment of vegan bias is not usual in the eating disorder field. As a result, vegans cannot take for granted that their vegan concerns will be heard by professionals.

Professional bias may relate to many topics. Fuller and Hill apply the acronym "social GRACES," which was "developed for clinicians to be aware of the many areas in life where we may have conscious or unconscious bias in clinical work." The acronym currently includes "gender, geography, race, religion, age, ability, appearance, class, culture, ethnicity, education, employment, sexuality, sexual orientation and spirituality," and the authors suggest adding "diet and dietary choice" (2021, p. 97). The counseling ethical principle of "justice," which the ACA (2014, p. 3) defines as "treating individuals equitably and fostering fairness and equality," may serve as a foundation upon which this "social grace" is added. So the values underlying veganism's dietary component must be understood by the clinician to allow optimal validation of the patient's experience. Tammy Beasley, MS, RDN, CEDS-S, LD, says,

> We can't tell clients that their relationship with food is unique, valid, and about nourishing the whole person AND make them throw away something as valued and important as veganism is for some people—simply because we, ourselves, do not understand or agree with it.
>
> (Beasley, 2020)

During my counseling graduate training, I learned to reflect deeply on any part of myself that might interfere with a client's treatment. I consulted with my professors and clinical supervisors when I encountered difficulty in applying this reflexivity in practice. Supervision is a safe space to discuss subjects such as unconscious bias with experienced professionals. I was made aware that supervisory consultation ideally continues throughout a therapist's career.

If a non-vegan therapist has not acknowledged their feelings about animal consumption, this lack of acknowledgment risks showing up— however passively, however unspoken—in the room with a vegan client. Professionals may think that by virtue of the therapeutic relationship, such a risk would not exist—after all, it is a completely different relationship than with friends or family—but that is an assumption made at a client's risk. According to Wosket,

> An important part of the work that a counsellor needs to undertake in their personal therapy and supervision is a sifting through of [their] own psychologically determined responses and a rigorous examination of how these may impact on their counselling work.
>
> (1999, Kindle location 764)

Therapists draw upon different therapeutic modalities in their work with clients. It may be useful to draw from some of these modalities when addressing one's own unconscious bias about veganism.

A psychodynamic therapist often supports their client in bringing unconscious material into conscious awareness. In doing so, the client may become aware of certain defenses and subsequently access their own agency. In a similar way, the therapist works with their own supervisor and/or personal therapist to access unconscious material of their own. A cognitive-behavioral therapist might support an eating disorder patient in recognizing their "automatic thoughts" (Gillihan, 2018, p. 7), just as the therapist may challenge their own automatic thoughts. In much the same way that a therapist drawing from acceptance and commitment therapy might encourage a patient to identify their values, so too might the therapist draw on ACT's principles to identify their own. As therapists in general encourage patients to continually assess their motivation, so too might therapists continually assess their own. By extension, therapists who have gone through their own processes regarding veganism may model healthful processing for their patients.

Clients and therapists alike can resist change. According to Rogers,

> If you are willing to enter [a patient's] private world and see the way life appears to him without any attempt to make evaluative judgments, you run the risk of being changed yourself. You might see it his way. You might find yourself influenced in your attitudes or personality. The risk of being changed is one of the most frightening prospects most of us can face.
>
> (Rogers, 1961, p. 333)

Therefore, just as therapists encourage clients to face their resistance, so too can they benefit from addressing their own, especially if doing so will serve as the route toward supporting the client in the way they need to be supported.

Reframing Cognitive Distortions

In his book *Cognitive Behavioral Therapy Made Simple*, Gillihan (2018) summarizes a previously developed list of "cognitive distortions" originally developed by psychiatrists Aaron T. Beck and David D. Burns. Let us now explore how certain cognitive distortions, as outlined by Gillihan, might play out within a professional who is unaware of their vegan bias.

Fortune-Telling

One such cognitive distortion is "fortune telling," which means "making predictions based on scant information" (Gillihan, 2018, p. 57). Professionals see this as a cognitive distortion when clients do it, and they aim to treat it. However, professionals are not immune to fortune-telling when it comes to veganism and its role in the client's life. It is important that therapists do not fill in gaps on their own; they need to become consciously informed. What constitutes "informed"? This is a question that professionals must continually ask themselves as they acquire more information, just like any other evolving therapeutic area.

Black-and-White Thinking

Black-and-white thinking, which means "seeing things in extreme terms" (Gillihan, 2018, p. 57), is another cognitive distortion in which professionals may engage as they consider an eating disordered client's veganism. It is important that therapists identify when they are engaging in this distortion. Might there be room to consider different aspects of a patient's veganism when planning their treatment (as discussed in Chapter 4)? Might there be room to consider that therapists might be putting eating disordered vegan patients into a "veganism equals restriction" box, end of story?

The moment therapists acknowledge that it is possible to both be ethically vegan and have an eating disorder is the moment they are forced to hold these two realities at once and forge a level of acceptance that veganism is a valid, conceivable, and executable principle in its own right. The concept of veganism becomes humanized in that sense and thus harder to automatically pin on the eating disorder. It is newly possible for these two seemingly polarized realities to co-exist with one another. For a therapist who believes that veganism is totally negative in recovery, this can be a hard pill to swallow. It is therefore imperative that therapists themselves seek the necessary support in holding these two realities at once.

My training has taught me that a therapist is capable of holding space for that which is both true and untrue at the same time. For example, a client may say something that is true for them but which the therapist may believe is only a part of the story. It is okay for the therapist to hold both thoughts at once. A competent therapist can do this without compromising their authentic validation of the client's truth. Therapists have the trained ability and the subsequent responsibility to hold these two truths at once. The client may not be able to hold these truths in that moment, but the therapist can. The client may be stuck in all-or-nothing thinking, but the therapist need not be. The therapist is in the advantageous position of seeing the client in a broader, more multi-faceted way than the client is able to see for themselves. The therapist ought to use this position with care and regard the vegan client as a whole person who is capable of believing one thing now and another thing later. A therapist may attempt to guess what may unfold for the patient later, but in order to make even the most educated guess, the therapist must be with the client completely in the present moment. The moment a therapist makes unfounded claims or assumptions (however logical they may seem) about a client's future is the moment they stop being present with the client in the now. That is because formulating those claims necessitates a focus on something other than the client's present experience with the therapist. In doing this, the therapist makes a conscious choice to align with their own perspective, not their client's. If the idea is to arrive at an honest conclusion as treatment ensues, then therapists must listen honestly.

Overgeneralization

Another cognitive distortion is "overgeneralization," which means "believing that one instance applies to every situation" (Gillihan, 2018, p. 57). Therapists regard overgeneralization as a cognitive distortion when patients engage in it. By extension, it might also help to consider when their own beliefs are generalized without sufficient reasoning.

During treatment, an eating disorder client needs, more than at any other time, to be regarded as a person first. It is therefore essential that the eating disorder is regarded secondarily to the person. The non-vegan therapist–vegan patient relationship may present certain challenges on its own, but when an eating disorder is in the mix, it is essential for a therapist to be alert to any unconscious bias. Neglecting to do so could negatively impact the course of the vegan patient's treatment.

April Lang, LCSW, SEP, in addressing therapists of vegan clients, says that therapists:

> must realize that when working with vegan clients, there's a good chance that at some point they will be discussing situations of extreme animal cruelty and abuse, possibly eliciting strong reactions in us . . . it's possible you might feel defensive. Unless the client is overtly judging you, your reaction could be due to an unconscious awareness that even though you're a compassionate person in so many ways, your actions towards non-human animals might not always be aligned with that part of you . . . Unfortunately many people still harbor negative stereotypes about veganism and if you have had little or no association with vegans and/or fully understand their lifestyle, you too may have internalized an unfavorable opinion of these clients.
> (A. Lang, personal communication, January 27, 2021)

A substantial portion of therapeutic work can be done before a clinician even enters the room. The path will be much clearer if the therapist has first examined their own beliefs about veganism. Just as therapists encourage clients to separate the eating disorder from veganism, just as therapists want clients to move away from veganism if it is found to be a part of the disorder, just as therapists work with clients to help them personally arrive at the right conclusion, so too must therapists separate the field's overarching view from their own.

To Simultaneously Know and Not Know

A major pitfall of non-vegan care for a vegan patient is that on the one hand, vegans need professionals to understand the vegan-specific aspects of their struggle—not necessarily fully, as I've mentioned, but at least to a degree that will allow alignment with the patient, e.g., in the form of a therapeutic alliance.

Now, let us consider our ability, as humans, to know while, at the same time, not invest ourselves in knowing. This can work to our benefit in preventing us from merging with another person or carrying their emotional burden. However, if we really got to know the vegan patient's position within non-vegan treatment—if we really validated their feelings on the subject—we might reason that the vegan person ought not be in this position.

This is where we get stuck. This right here is the crux of the issue. If a professional tries to understand, then their understanding may, just may, lead to a change of heart about the patient's meal determination (just like the vegan had a change of heart when they let themselves understand the plights of animals). If eating disorder professionals understand enough to see why this particular change may help the person, then they risk understanding past their own comfort level.

Professionals who believe that the vegan patient would benefit from a vegan approach may in part regard this belief as beneficient. However, it may also seem unfathomable that a vegan approach could be beneficient. So in an effort to "do no harm," professionals might keep things as they are. In this way, one ethical principle is traded for another. Nonmaleficence is compromised for the sake of supposed beneficence, which, in this case, takes the form of things staying the same. The statement "I can see why their current situation poses damage" is incompatible with the statement "Things will remain as they are." This incompatibility serves as a block toward patient advocacy. For a vegan, there isn't a way to make these two things fit together—that is, the simultaneous *understanding* of the way things are and the *commitment* to the way things are. Patients can, therefore, only be safely understood up to a point. They can only be met part of the way—notably not "where they are," which, as we've said, is pivotal to effective treatment.

Vegan patients, like all patients, need and deserve to be met where they are. And without a vegan-informed framework within which to navigate, a professional who has had little exposure to veganism may be treading in unfamiliar territory without a map.

References

American Counseling Association. (2014). *2014 ACA code of ethics.* www.counseling.org/docs/default-source/default-document-library/2014-code-of-ethics-finaladdress.pdf

Beasley, T. (R. D. N.) (2020, May 15). *Veganism and eating disorder recovery.* Alsana®. Retrieved April 7, 2022, from www.alsana.com/blog/eating-disorder-recovery-bringing-vegans-into-the-fold/

Fuller, S. J., & Hill, K. M. (2021). Attitudes toward veganism in eating disorder professionals. *BJPsych Bulletin, 46*(2), 95–99. doi: 10.1192/bjb.2021.57

Gillihan, S. J. (2018). *Cognitive behavioral therapy made simple: 10 strategies for managing anxiety, depression, anger, panic, and worry.* Althea Press.

Rogers, C. R. (1961). *On becoming a person: A therapist's view on psychotherapy.* Houghton Mifflin.

Wosket, V. (1999). *The therapeutic use of self: Counselling practice, research and supervision.* Routledge.

18

PROPOSING A VEGAN-INFORMED APPROACH

The culmination of this book is a proposal for a vegan-informed approach to care. The "vegan-informed" term is adapted from the "trauma-informed" approach. I draw from the trauma-informed approach because it takes into account that patients with trauma histories will simply not receive neutral treatment if professionals do not consciously consider their specialized needs. To the contrary, there is real potential for harm. The Center for Substance Abuse (US) states, "The ethical principle, 'first, do no harm,' resonates strongly in the application of TIC [Trauma Informed Care]". The proposal for a vegan-informed model speaks to this book's main aim of prioritizing beneficence and nonmaleficence. What I suggest is a rubric that would need to be researched in hopes of being regarded as evidence based.

DOI: 10.4324/9781003310617-22

A vegan informed model is based on a trauma-informed one but does not inherently presume trauma in vegans. That said, veganism is complex. There are many reasons a vegan person may feel traumatized, including existing co-morbid trauma in which issues around boundaries, attachment, abandonment, merging, etc. may overlap with a vegan's experience of aligning with vegan values. There may be vegan-related trauma that has nothing to do with trauma in other life areas. There may be trauma related to witnessing violence done to animals in a variety of mediums. I am adapting from the trauma-informed model because I believe its fundamental framework can be reasonably adapted toward helping vegans with their own unique needs.

Additionally, let us consider those eating disordered individuals who have histories of trauma. If a proportion of these individuals are vegan, then there is a strong likelihood that their need for trauma-informed care will coincide with their need for vegan-informed care. Both the vegan-informed and trauma-informed models will work in tandem with one another when implemented together. That said, harm can be done if trauma-informed care is implemented but vegan-informed care is not. So again, this model would serve as neutral at worst (to draw from when needed) and helpful at best, whereas its absence could be detrimental to those who need, but do not receive, suitable care.

This vegan-informed model, as predicated on the reasoning throughout this book, raises veganism to a level of equal consideration to that of non-veganism; hence why I emphasize a vegan-related rationale (rather than a non-vegan-related rationale). Vegans need vegan-specific help in order to optimally recover, whereas non-vegans do not need vegan-specific help. This is why I wish to highlight the *existence* of vegan consideration; it is why I depict a vegan perspective only as it pertains to a vegan framework. That said, I explicitly hold that *non-vegan experiences count just as much as vegan experiences.* By extension, non-vegans' quality of care is equally as important as vegans' quality of care. Professionals who are vegan-informed are better equipped to navigate the emotions of vegans, non-vegans, vegetarians, etc. that may come up around this topic.

Existing Frameworks

I will combine elements of the following trauma-informed sources to form a unique vegan-informed model:

1. The Substance Abuse and Mental Health Services Administration's (SAMHSA, 2014) "six fundamental principles" of the trauma-informed approach: safety; trustworthiness and transparency; peer support; collaboration and mutuality; empowerment, voice, and choice; and cultural, historical, and gender issues.

2. The Center for Substance Abuse Treatment's application of a trauma-informed approach to behavioral health settings lists the following: trauma awareness and understanding; recognize that trauma-related symptoms and behaviors originate from adapting to traumatic experiences; view trauma in the context of individuals' environments; minimize the risk of retraumatization or replicating prior trauma dynamics; create a safe environment; identify recovery from trauma as a primary goal; support control, choice, and autonomy; create collaborative relationships and participation opportunities; familiarize the client with trauma-informed services; incorporate universal routine screenings for trauma; view trauma through a sociocultural lens; use a strengths-focused perspective; promote resilience; foster trauma-resistant skills; demonstrate organizational and administrative commitment to TIC; develop strategies to address secondary trauma and promote self-care; provide hope—recovery is possible.

A Prospective Vegan-Informed Approach

1. Promote Trauma Awareness and Understanding

(The Center for Substance Abuse Treatment, US; principle: Trustworthiness and Transparency (SAMHSA, 2014))

A vegan-informed approach would begin by clearly defining ethical veganism. From this foundation, internal training and supervision on veganism and ongoing conversations with a facility's own clinicians will develop an understanding. As mental health staff become informed about exactly what veganism is, they will be better able to distinguish between "true" vegan patients and patients who may not be vegan in principle. If they can better distinguish veganism from an eating disordered mentality that is "using" veganism, they would be better informed to know what questions to ask a vegan eating disordered client. Staff may also benefit from knowing about the animal-agriculture industry practices so that they might know what clients are referencing when talking about animal mistreatment.

Vegan clients should never feel pressured to prove the existence of animals' mistreatment to staff. Instead, there can be an honest conversation about the vegan person's alignment to their values in either dietary or non-dietary ways. An understanding of the facts on which vegan values are based will provide staff with the best possible information to guide patients. In essence, staff and vegan clients will be speaking the same language.

Staff can certainly ask a vegan client to explain why they find fault with animal-agriculture practices to get to know the person better. Research mentioned in Chapter 2 found that patients wanted to be regarded as "whole people." In that vein, so long as these questions are asked in the interest of getting to know the patient as a whole person, then it may be fine to ask for elaboration upon why they believe what they do. (See also Chapter 14's discussion on congruence.) And as with any other question concerning a client's beliefs, the client should be met with non-judgment no matter their answer.

2. Create a Safe Environment

(Center for Substance Abuse Treatment; principle: Safety (SAMHSA, 2014))
This trauma-informed principle ensures that "interpersonal interactions promote a sense of safety." Additionally, according to SAMHSA (2014), "understanding safety as defined by those served is a high priority." A vegan-informed model may adapt SAMHSA's "safety" principle by ensuring that interactions about veganism entail empathic, nonjudgmental listening. When applicable, professionals would proactively consider a vegan patient's experience of being in a primarily non-vegan treatment environment. A safe treatment environment would

allow space for the vegan patient to process any feelings that come up around veganism in individual or group therapy sessions.

Ongoing work on the part of professionals is important to ensure the safety and effectiveness of a client's treatment. Bear in mind that this patient is struggling with the vegan components of their treatment and that getting through a non-vegan meal presents a unique challenge, one that is wholly unrelated to their eating disorder. This struggle means that a therapist should simultaneously view this person's treatment through two separate lenses: an eating disorder lens and a vegan lens. The vegan eating disordered client needs treatment providers to consider their eating disorder *and* their veganism at every step of their treatment.

3. View Trauma in the Context of Individuals' Environments

(The Center for Substance Abuse Treatment, US)

A vegan-informed model would regard vegans through the lens of veganism rather than through the lens of a non-vegan treatment norm (as discussed in Chapter 15). This would involve incorporating the vegan perspective discussed most prominently in Chapters 8, 9, and 10.

4. Minimize the Risk of Retraumatization or Replicating Prior Trauma Dynamics

(The Center for Substance Abuse Treatment, US; principle: Understanding, SAMHSA, 2014)

In vegan-informed terms, this would refer to discussions in Chapters 7 through 10 about vegan-related trauma. Minimizing the risk of such trauma would involve understanding it as distinctly vegan trauma (while also allowing space for other types of trauma that may or may not relate to the vegan trauma) and then, being mindful of a possible retraumatizing effect of eating non-vegan food. As discussed in Chapter 10, vegans may also be retraumatized by having to adopt a detached state or grapple with cognitive dissonance in non-vegan settings with animal therapy. Minimizing the risk of vegan-related retraumatization would involve considering the ways a vegan person may have experienced trauma in the process of becoming vegan (discussed in Chapter 7). This trauma may include the vicarious trauma of seeing someone else hurt, in this case animals. It may also include hearing someone else's story of witnessing harm done to animals.

Minimizing risk of vegan-related retraumatization would entail prioritizing the formation of an early therapeutic alliance (discussed in Chapter 14). It would also entail, as in the trauma-informed model, being aware of the professionals with whom the patient has shared their vegan experience. This would go hand in hand with the importance of staff communication within, across, and throughout varying levels of care, as discussed in Chapter 16. When all team members are on the same page about the significance of the person's veganism, the patient might not have to repeat the same story to different people. Not having to repeat the story may help the patient avoid unnecessarily reigniting the story's accompanying feelings. Also, it may be a relief for a patient to know they don't have to repeat their story to "convince" each professional individually that their veganism is significantly important to them. Rather, the patient can trust that all members of the team have been adequately informed by others responsible for their care.

5. Identify Recovery From Trauma as a Primary Goal

(The Center for Substance Abuse Treatment, US)

In vegan eating disorder patients, a vegan-informed approach would "identify recovery from an *eating disorder* as a primary goal." Those under the impression that letting go of veganism is in itself an indicator of recovery (the flip side of thinking that adopting veganism is a possible indicator of an eating disorder, as discussed in Chapter 3) are missing the point. This is because veganism itself is not the point, whether in reference to getting sicker or getting better.

For an eating disordered patient using veganism as a ruse, forgoing vegan eating in itself is not a recovery marker. We must separate "vegan" from "the thing that improved eating disorder recovery outcome." For this patient, realizing that veganism had been an expression of their disorder may lead toward recovery. Like any distorted belief influencing an eating disordered person, letting it go is absolutely a movement toward recovery. In this case, the patient has let go of a false conviction of veganism. I say good for them, but they did not let go of true veganism. In the opposite case, someone who remains vegan in values but not in diet did not forgo veganism to recover. That is to say, they did not suddenly stop caring about the ethical treatment of animals. They simply did whatever they considered practicably possible in alignment with their values.

6. Support Control, Choice, and Autonomy

(The Center for Substance Abuse Treatment, US; principle: Empowerment, Voice, and Choice (SAMHSA, 2014))

Vegan-informed treatment would offer as much control, choice, and autonomy as is "practicably possible" to the vegan eating disordered patient. This, of course, varies from one patient to the next as well as from the truly-vegan patient to the not-truly-vegan patient. It also varies from one treatment center to the next and from one level of care to the next. Vegan-informed care would state that, to the extent that it can be done, it ought to be done. Therefore, every possible step should be taken to the farthest extent in treatment. This notion relates to the discussion of assessments—and continual assessments throughout treatment—from Chapter 12 and the discussion of ambivalence in Chapter 13.

7. Create Collaborative Relationships and Participation Opportunities

(The Center for Substance Abuse Treatment, US; principle: Collaboration and Mutuality (SAMHSA, 2014))

In vegan-informed care, this could reference the practices from Chapter 15 including collaborative cooking groups and restaurant outings. This principle can also center around the therapeutic alliance (discussed in Chapter 14), as the concept of this alliance is based on the idea that the therapist–client relationship is a collaboration, wherein each person's perspectives inform the conversations and outcomes. It may be useful to build organizational collaboration on the collaborative as well as personalized nature of the therapeutic alliance.

8. Familiarize the Client With Trauma-Informed Services

(The Center for Substance Abuse Treatment, US; principle: Peer Support (SAMHSA, 2014))

For vegan-informed care, this could mean suggesting vegan resources that may help patients align with their vegan values as they recover. For example, vegan patients may attend a vegan support group or join a vegan advocacy community. Treatment providers may work with vegan patients to explore how different kinds of support might be beneficial to their recovery. The vegan advocacy organization, In Defense of Animals, offers an animal-activist support group for vegans. Valerie Martin, LCSW, offers a monthly vegan support group.[1] Additionally, vegan food, cooking, baking, restaurant, and nutrition resources may be helpful to a vegan person in recovery via increased socialization, working through food challenges, and growing their knowledge about nutrition.

9. Incorporate Universal Routine Screenings for Trauma

(The Center for Substance Abuse Treatment, US)

For vegan-informed care, this would refer to the various types of assessments discussed in Chapter 12, ideally given throughout the duration of treatment, and the discussion of ambivalence in Chapter 13.

10. View Trauma Through a Sociocultural Lens

(The Center for Substance Abuse Treatment, US; principle: Cultural, Historical, and Gender Issues (SAMHSA, 2014))

For vegan-informed care, this refers to various elements of the person's sociocultural identity, as discussed in Chapter 11. Different vegans relate to a vegan identity differently, and different vegans have different sociocultural backgrounds, including different gender, racial, and/or religious identities that may shape their identity as vegans, their relationship to veganism, and the process they underwent in becoming vegan. Sociocultural factors may

1 Support Resources Mentioned: https://idausa.org/campaign/sustainable-activism/events/; Valerie Martin offers a monthly vegan support group: https://veganandvibrant.com/supportgroup

influence how accepted their veganism was in their families, friendship groups, relationships, and broader communities. All these factors may influence how a vegan is affected by the non-vegan components of treatment and the potential for vegan-related retraumatization.

11. Use a Strengths-Focused Perspective: Promote Resilience

(Center for Substance Abuse, US)

In a vegan-informed context, this refers to Chapter 13's discussion about considering veganism openly and curiously. Staff may consider using the value-derived language vegans use, e.g., "What is practicably possible for you?" rather than "What can't/shouldn't you do?" It is not necessary to use this language verbatim, although it may certainly help. The more important element is the professional's mindset. If the staff member has this language in mind, they can demonstrate alignment with the patient's veganism and, in doing so, help that patient feel met where they are. This can help the patient connect to their strengths, abilities, and potential to recover, even if their treatment involves making decisions that are out of alignment with their vegan values.

Promoting strength and resilience also refers to, where applicable, fostering a patient's ability to go out into the world as a person in recovery and being able to handle the non-vegan aspects of the world as they encounter them. Resilience helps them exercise the flexibility necessary with eating disorder recovery in a vegan context (this would refer to Chapter 6's discussion of vegans' understanding that they live in a primarily non-vegan world). It focuses on maintaining that the eating disorder is the issue at hand. Resilience helps the patient proactively determine how veganism will fit into their vision of recovery. It helps them remember who they are and how they may feel strengthened by their vegan values. How can they assert themselves in the world as a vegan?

This can be done with eating disordered symptoms in the same way that non-vegan eating disorder treatment can. This can also look like a professional asking a vegan patient, on vegan terms, "What is practicably possible for you?" "What can you do to practice your values?" For some, this may include eating a fully vegan diet; for others, it may involve eating a partially vegan diet while living in accordance with veganism in other ways. These suggestions can fall into two categories: *refrainment* and *action*. For example, a vegan person can *refrain* from purchasing household items that were tested on animals or take *action* by volunteering at a farm sanctuary. They can also learn how to communicate their vegan ethics to others, which can also serve to improve their therapeutic interpersonal effectiveness skills.

A strengths-based approach for vegan eating disorder patients may involve helping them become creative with cooking and baking, accompanying them to grocery stores during treatment to point out the challenging vegan foods and ingredients, and incorporating those foods and ingredients into cooking groups and restaurant outings.

12. Develop Strategies to Address Secondary Trauma and Promote Self-Care

(The Center for Substance Abuse Treatment, US)

In a vegan-informed approach, secondary trauma could take the form of eating or being exposed to others' eating and discussing non-vegan food in treatment. Chapter 9 discussed non-vegan food as akin to medicine; Chapter 10 discussed the contradiction between a horse's/dog's aliveness and a cow/pig's deadness. Professionals can help by attending to these often confusing, unsettling, and painful aspects of a vegan's experience.

13. Provide Hope

(Center for Substance Abuse, US; principle: Recovery Is Possible (SAMHSA, 2014).

In vegan-informed terms, this would mean providing hope for eating disorder recovery in every patient. Patients have the best chance at aligning with that hope if they are supported in all of the above ways.

In Sum

This model is meant to be a reference. Its components can serve as a baseline from which to apply it uniquely to different patients. But at the very least,

I believe the model needs to exist. We need to create space for the option that veganism could be authentic and, furthermore, that it could be feasible. Within this space, we can take actionable steps towards a vegan patient's betterment.

References

Center for Substance Abuse Treatment (US). Trauma-Informed Care in Behavioral Health Services. Rockville (MD): Substance Abuse and Mental Health Services Administration (US). (2014). *Trauma-informed care: A sociocultural perspective* (Treatment Improvement Protocol (TIP) Series, No. 57.) Chapter 1. www.ncbi.nlm.nih.gov/books/NBK207195/

SAMHSA's Concept of Trauma and Guidance for a Trauma-Informed Approach | SAMHSA Publications and Digital Products. (2014). *Publications and digital products*. Retrieved April 3, 2022, from https://store.samhsa.gov/product/SAMHSA-s-Concept-of-Trauma-and-Guidance-for-a-Trauma-Informed-Approach/SMA14-4884

CONCLUSION

Considering the global increase in eating disorders and veganism, it is imperative to bring the topic of veganism and eating disorders to the fore. This topic has long been discussed, but much of the discussion has been based on negative presumptions about veganism. The eating disorder field has defaulted to erring on the side of caution for a vegan eating disordered client. The negativity surrounding this topic has very real implications for eating disordered individuals and the field in general. Currently espoused views often minimize, dismiss, or simply do not make room for the whole of an eating disordered vegan person's experience. Remaining complacent in the current view closes off opportunities to the eating disorder field as they provide vegan eating disordered individuals with the support that they need at all levels of care. Due to the increase in both eating disorders and veganism, I reason that the field has a responsibility to expand its perspective on this topic. It is time to proactively assess veganism's presence within the eating disorder field.

As seen throughout this book, there have been many inconsistencies in the trajectory from research to practice. Many mainstream views of veganism have been conveyed in confusing and contradictory manners toward their intended audience. Recipients of these messages are thus

DOI: 10.4324/9781003310617-23

potentially being presented with misleading or incomplete information about veganism and are therefore not in an ideal position to draw reliable conclusions or accurate perceptions concerning those who are both vegan and eating disordered.

The field would do well by vegan patients to pause between hearing the word "veganism" and concluding its negative implications for an eating disordered individual. Within that pause, there exists space for myriad possibilities. In this book, I have attempted to bring attention to one of these possibilities, namely that veganism is not fundamentally synonymous with or indicative of eating disordered restriction. Once we create space for that possibility to exist, we can begin to have a true client-focused conversation.

That conversation might entail obstacles. This is okay—good, in fact, because we should be (continually) addressing the obstacles and coming to honest, thorough conclusions. These obstacles may be organizational (e.g., funding), dietary (e.g., nutritional needs), or personal (e.g., unprocessed feelings about veganism). I have intentionally abstained from proposing concrete, one-size-fits-all conclusions—either for the profession as a whole demographic or for patients as a whole demographic. I refrain from making sweeping generalizations and instead propose that therapists should focus on practicing the ethical principles of beneficence and nonmaleficence in ways that can only be determined on a case-by-case basis. I suggest that solutions to treating vegans in eating disorder centers may begin with curiosity. What information is out there about veganism and eating disorders? How might this information play a role in our perception? How can we deepen our understanding of a vegan person's experience? Moreover, how can we acknowledge that we know the answer only *after* getting a sense of that particular patient's needs?

Veganism and eating disorders are wholly seperate concepts unto themselves. It is important to recognize when aspects of each concept, such as perfectionism and all-or-nothing thinking, are mistakenly conflated with one another. If we can recognize these concepts for what they are, then we can reliably surmise when they are being conflated by a patient. If we can work toward identifying this conflation, then we will be better positioned to help patients in the way they need us to help them.

I have explored possible traumatic ramifications of a vegan eating disordered person eating non-vegan meals. A vegan's ability to practice mindfulness while eating might be automatically compromised when presented with non-vegan food. There may even be a traumatic reaction. When professionals mistake this reaction for an eating disordered reaction, it can compound the patient's already-unnecessary suffering. This missed signal can pose severe detriment to a patient. It is thus essential to build in appropriate understanding and support for this patient. This discomfort also applies to treatment involving the presence of both therapy animals and food animals. The vegan patient recognizes an overt display of cognitive dissonance around them and needs a way to process this safely.

There are open and flexible ways forward. Even the most concrete pieces of information I have put forth are embedded with flexibility and thoughtfulness when considering the best route for each individual patient. The assessments and approaches in this book are vegan-informed. At best, they could truly benefit a patient. At worst, they are neutral. While they might not automatically lead to a patient's recovery, at the very least, they do not impose harm to the patient. There is no harm in incorporating the knowledge that veganism is distinct from eating disorders into one's work with a patient, but there can be potential harm in not doing so. The eating disorder field would do well to implement psychological principles, including assessment of professional unconscious bias, at the basis of their practice.

Helping vegans does not automatically entail allowing them to be vegan in treatment, but it does mean refraining from prematurely closing off that option. A vegan's experience and internal world must be considered. A vegan's reality must be legitimized in the eating disorder community if we are to have honest, open, and unbiased discourse about how to treat a patient who lives according to vegan values.

Furthermore, refusing to admit people into a treatment center on the basis of their veganism can have negative effects on both "true" vegans and eating disordered people restricting in the name of veganism. How can the former person hope to recover if their values misalign with treatment's standards? And how can the latter person get a chance to realize this if not first being allowed in the door? If all the client can see is that they are not being "allowed" to eat what they want, they may not arrive at the honest conclusion that what they "want" is not what they need. For the person whose veganism is a guise for an eating disorder, they deserve an opportunity to explore the underpinnings of their stated preference and ultimately do what is best for their recovery.

There is a way forward here. And it includes patients who are vegan, patients who are not vegan, patients who later realize that their veganism was an eating disorder guise, and patients who maintain their ethical stances over the long-term. This is a shift that takes clients' needs into account on every possible level. It therefore applies to everyone.

A vegan in recovery needs their recovery approach to grow with them. They need treatment to make appropriate adaptations toward their vegan-related needs. What happens then, when recovery decisions do not match the rate of their growth or do not adapt to their new perspectives? Patients on the receiving end of professional assumptions about their veganism may experience treatment as stationary rather than progressive. Patients whose vegan needs are not being met in adaptation may experience treatment as rejection. It is therefore time for the eating disorder field to acknowledge the possibility that on both an individual and organizational level, what might have worked in the past may not necessarily work in the present. From there, it may adequately self-assess its vegan-related perspectives and subsequent treatment approaches.

We have already broken through so many barriers in the eating disorder treatment field. We already know so much about matters that have formerly misled us. And yet here we are, with a deepened understanding of eating disorders and a subsequent ability to help many who are suffering. I am hopeful that, by continuing to broaden our understanding, we can co-facilitate this shift.

A coffee, a cake, a conversation

I would like to end this book on a personal note. In the book's preface, I mentioned Valerie Martin, the "vegan therapist" whose blog post about her experience as a vegan in the therapy field further fueled my passion for this project. Just knowing that someone else was out there doing this work gave me immense hope for the potential of our field. I also felt like I suddenly wasn't alone in how I felt!

Valerie and I had a few phone and internet conversations over the past couple of years, loosely staying on one another's radar. She even had me on her vegan podcast, where we spoke about this book and about veganism in general. Well, it so happened that I recently got to meet Valerie in person during her trip to New York City. If you must know (because I know you're all dying to know), we went to Central Park and drank lattes and ate mini carrot cakes. It was a lovely, warm, happy, spontaneous outing. We bonded as friends, as vegans, and as therapists. And while we were sitting on a rock in Central Park, eating our cake and drinking our lattes, I finally got to thank her in person for her part in inspiring this work.

The connection that I formed with Valerie speaks so clearly to the connection I have intended to foster with this book. It is an open kind of connection, an ongoing conversation, a meeting of the minds and hearts. It is also a testament to the part of myself that loves connecting authentically with others, and to that end, a testament to my own eating disorder recovery, which allows that part of me to feel alive!

I want every eating disorder patient, vegan or not, to sit on some rock in some park with some friend eating some cake. (The latte is optional.) I want that kind of eating disorder freedom to be available to everyone, including vegans. I hope the information contained within these pages has offered a foundation on which to bring vegans into the conversation and, in kind, cultivate their potential to obtain eating disorder freedom.

INDEX

Acceptance and Commitment
Therapy (ACT) 132–133, 160
Accanto Health 4, 48
Adams, C. J. 71, 73, 78
Alaska Eating Disorders Alliance
29–31
Alsana i, 22, 39, 43, 48, 147
"alternative food network" 37
American Counseling Association
(ACA) 2–3, 159
American Journal of Clinical
Nutrition 23
American Psychiatric Association
(APA) 6
American Psychological Association
(APA) 2
Andersen, S. T. 22
anorexia nervosa (AN) 6, 22, 29–31,
89–90
Anxiety and Depression Association
of America (ADAA) 29
asceticism 123
Aspen, V. 106, 136

assessments 90, 108, 131, 179; in
communication 156; continual
assessments 121, 172; with
eating disordered patients
132; nutritional assessment
118; standardized assessment
considerations 121–124; of vegan
bias 159
authentic eating disorder
identity 108
Avoidant/Restrictive Food Intake
Disorder (ARFID) 6

BALANCE Eating Disorder
Treatment Center 4, 22, 67, 114
Bardone-Cone, A. M. 54–55
Barnett, M. J. 37
Barrington Behavioral Health and
Wellness 29–30
Barthels, F. 51
Beasley, T. 21, 39, 43, 48–49,
113–114, 116, 121, 146–147, 159
Beck, Aaron T. 161

Begeny, C. T. 135
Beglin 122
Berg 122
binge eating disorder (BED) 6, 29–31
black-and-white thinking 161–162
Blomquist, K. K. 37
Boswell, Megan 117
Briones, Jasmine 38
Brown, A. 6, 22, 24, 43, 118
Brunner, Emmy 43
Brytek-Matera, A. 37, 50–51
bulimia nervosa (BN) 6, 29–31
Burns, David D. 161

Cabaniss, D. L. 139
Cassin 134
Center for Discovery 30–31, 92
Center for Substance Abuse
    Treatment 166, 168–175
Chandler, C. K. 96–97, 99
Charles 49
Çiçekoğlu, P. 52
client/patient 2; accepting 43; ACT
    approach 133; animals and,
    relationship between 97; assessing
    116; assessment of 130; black-and-
    white thinking of 161–162; clinical
    determination about 3; cognitive
    distortion 161; communication to
    156–157; continual assessments
    121; conversation with 178;
    diet mentality 34–35; eating
    disordered clients 21–23, 87,
    91–92, 141–142, 169–170; ethical
    components of 65; familiarizing
    trauma-informed services to 173;
    forced regression experience by
    99; goal of 131; individual needs
    3–5, 132, 148–149; individual
    outpatient treatment 153–154;
    inpatient treatment 155; intensive
    outpatient treatment 154–155;

loss of identity in 92–93;
mindfulness versus dissociation
79–84; non-vegan therapist–vegan
patient relationship 163–164;
outpatient treatment 21;
perception of disorder 22,
122–123; perspective on 19;
reality, questioning 48–55; in
recovery 4; resisting change 160;
restriction in the view of 39; staff
and 169; therapeutic alliance and
142–144; therapeutic relationship
with 139–140, 142–144, 147, 159;
therapist–client relationship 172;
trauma ties of 93–94; treatment
centers' non-acceptance of 42–43;
"treatment team" 8; triggers
in 40–42; trusted revelation of
authentic values 140; veganism
of, professionally considering
113–124; vegan patient 44–45;
vegan patient's unnecessary
work 84; vegan-related pain 79;
vegetarian patient 44–45
Cognitive Behavioral Therapy Made
    Simple 161
cognitive distortions, reframing 161
Comer, L. K. 53
communication 156–157
comorbid trauma 93–94
Consortium for Animal Assisted
    Therapy 99
Costin, C. 66, 79
counseling 15–16
Crowther, J. H. 122
Curtis, M. J. 53
Cypress Magazine 29–30

Dahlgren, C. L. 122
Dennett, Carrie i, viii
Diagnostic and Statistical Manual of
    Mental Disorders (DSM-5) 6

dietitian 8, 18, 155
Dripps, W. R. 37

Eating Attitudes Test (EAT-26) 122
eating disorder 16; anorexia 31;
    assessments 123; binge eating
    disorder 30–31; bulimia 30–31;
    closed versus open 36; defining
    6; Eating Disorder Inventory
    3 (EDI-3) 122; "ego-syntonic/
    dystonic" nature of 127–129;
    food as medicine 86–90;
    identification 105–106; indicator
    27–32; individual differences 105;
    mindset 35–36; misconceptions
    in 34–35; morality of 64–66;
    non-negotiables 38–39; orthorexia
    30–31; orthorexia and ethics
    55–56; reality 48–55; recovering
    from 66–68, 87; recovery from
    44–45; self-imposed food
    rules 62; specific challenges
    134–135; symptoms 23, 108, 174;
    therapeutic alliance and 141–144;
    treatment 16–19; triggers 40–42;
    types of 8; vegan eating disorder
    sufferers 22; veganism and
    15–20, 32, 61–62; veganism's
    co-existence with 5; see also
    specific aspects/types
Eating Disorder Awareness Week
    2019 29
Eating Disorder Examination
    Questionnaire (EDE-Q) 122
Eating Disorder Hope 29–31
Eating Disorder Inventory 3 (EDI-3)
    assessment 122
eating disorder treatment 5,
    22, 38–43, 62, 113, 147;
    complementary treatments
    153; counseling 15–16; food
    as medicine 86–90; individual

outpatient treatment 153–154;
    individualized 10, 63; inpatient
    18, 153, 155; intensive outpatient
    treatment 154–155; levels of care
    (LoC) 8, 152; mindful presence
    with food 79–80; misguided
    34–35; non-negotiables in
    38–39; nonvegan aspect of
    24; non-vegan patients in 145;
    outpatient 21; professionals
    involved in 8; therapeutic
    alliance as foundational aspect
    of 141; treatment centers'
    non-acceptance of vegans 42–43;
    vegan person in 94, 100, 148,
    179; vegan support group within
    147; veganism and 15–20, 22, 48,
    68, 161; see also non-vegan eating
    disorder treatment
embodiment 90–91
Emily Program 4, 22, 48, 149
ethical philosophy, veganism as 5
ethics 7, 35, 55–56, 62, 65, 81, 104,
    108, 156

Fairburn, C. G. 122
Fairhaven Treatment Center 30–31
Family Caregiver Support 29
Faunalytics 73
Fernando, J. W. 135
fortune-telling 161
freedom 66–68
Friborg, O. 122
Fuller, S. 6, 119, 121, 131, 150, 159

Ganaway, Glen 98
Gander, M. 93
Garner, D. M. 122, 123–124
Geller, J. 38, 134
Gendlin, E. T. 109, 135, 139–140
Gillihan, S. J. 160–161, 163
Goodman, D. 37

Goodman, M. K. 37
Grabb, G. S. 79
Graves, T. A. 141
Green, Che 73

Hamilton, M. 55, 65, 81
Hamshaw, Gena 56
Hays, D. G. 122
health-versus-ethics
    distinction 55
Heiss, S. 53–54, 122
Henderson, Z. B. 66
Hill, K. M. 159
Hunnicutt, Carrie 43

identity/identification 103–109;
    eating disordered identification
    105–106; eating disorder
    individual differences 105;
    eating disorder rules and
    vegan "rules," difference
    107–109; vegan identification
    104; vegan individual differences
    103–104
inauthentic eating disorder
    identity 108
incorporating versus omitting
    35–36
indicator, eating disorder 27–32
individual outpatient treatment
    153–154
inpatient treatment 8, 18, 89,
    153, 155
intensive outpatient treatment
    (IOP) 149, 154–155
International Association for
    Relational Psychoanalysis and
    Psychotherapy (IARPP) 71

Jomaa, Rimaa Danielle 73
Jones, M. 24
Judge, M. 104, 135

Katella, K. 23
Kofsky, R. 38, 49, 118
Kubler-Ross, E. 88

Lang, April 143, 163
levels of care (LoC) 8, 152
Levinson, B. M. 96
lifeforward movement 109
Lin, L. 121
Livermore, California school district
    30–31
Luce, K. H. 122

Madan, Apoorva 74
Mann, Clare 42, 71, 74, 123
Martin, Valerie ix, 173, 180–181
Martin-Wagar, Caitlin 116
Meyers, L. 98–99
McDonald, B. 54, 72–75, 78, 93
Miller, W. R. 134
misconceptions: about
    veganism 36; eating disorder
    field's 2, 32; professional
    outcomes of 34–35
morality 64–66
motivation for veganism 47–56;
    ethical reasons 53; "health-
    motivation" category 52;
    importance of understanding
    47–56; patient's reality,
    questioning 48–55
motivational interviewing (MI) 134–136
Multi-Service Eating Disorders
    Association (MEDA) 30–31
Musby, Eva 88–89

National Eating Disorders
    Association (NEDA) 6, 8, 28, 55
non-vegan eating disorder
    treatment 77–84, 174, 180;
    animal therapy in 96–101;
    implications of 77–84;

mindfulness versus dissociation 79–84; vegan patient's unnecessary work 84
non-vegan-to-vegan process 81
Norwood, R. 51–52
nutritional field 4
Nussbaum, A. 92

Oliver, C. 91
orthorexia nervosa (ON) 6, 29, 30–31, 50–51, 52, 55–56
ORTO-11 tests 122
ORTO-15 tests 122
other specified feeding and eating disorder (OSFED) 6, 29–31
outpatient treatment 21, 152; individual 153–154; intensive 154–155
overcontrol 123

Panoff, L. 7
partial hospitalization 8
Paslakis, G. 54
patient see client/patient
Penelo, E. 122
perfectionism 61–63
pica 6
plant-based diet 7
professional outcomes of misconceptions 34–35
professional self reflective practice 158–165
psychodynamic therapy 16, 160
Psychology & Veganism 74
Purcell Lalonde, M. 106

Rafferty, Olivia 24
Raz, Shiri 5, 71, 73, 78
recovery 34–45, 67; aligning with one's true self in 109, 131; as attaining freedom 66–68; closed versus open 36; communication in 156–157; eating disorder non-negotiables 38–39; for an ethical vegan 63; "good versus bad food" mentality 66; imperfection as an aspect of 62; incorporating versus omitting 35–36; individuals' potential for 21; mindfulness versus dissociation 79–84; morality to food assigning 64; motivation in 56; perspectives 34–45; as primary goal 171–172; professional outcomes of misconceptions 34–35; readiness 23; recovery-oriented lens 49; selecting versus restricting 35–36; standard recovery 150; term description 7–8; therapeutic alliance in 141–142; treatment centers' non-acceptance of vegans 42–43; upon discharge 89; vegan in 100, 116, 121; veganism and vegetarianism 44–45; veganism and diet 36–38; veganism as a trigger 40–42; vegan-specific help in 167
residential treatment 8
restriction 2, 34–37, 42–43, 120, 178; accidental 116; anorexia and 31; dietary, benefits 121, 123; as eating disorder's priorities 127–128; as non-negotiable 38–39; veganism as 9, 44, 92
Rising, Dallas 72, 143, 149
Rogers, C. R. 132, 136, 139–140, 160
Rogers, Melainie 4, 114
Roncero, M. 128
Root of the Future 7
Rose, J. S. 122
rumination disorder 6

Salvia, Meg 118–119
Sandoz, E. K. 128, 133

Seeds of Hope 29–31
selecting versus restricting
    35–36
Setnick, Jessica 119
social effects of eating 121
standard recovery 150
standardized assessment
    considerations 121–124
Stanghellini, G. 64
Stein, K. F. 64
Steinbech, Jessica 117
Steptoe, A. 123
Substance Abuse and Mental
    Health Services Administration's
    (SAMHSA) 168–170,
    172–173, 175

Taft, C. 93
Termorshuizen, J. D. 23
therapeutic alliance 139–144;
    eating disorders and 141–142;
    formation 171–172; vegan
    eating disordered patients and
    142–144
therapist 4, 22; ACT approach
    133; in animal therapy 96–97;
    black-and-white thinking of
    161–162; client and, relationship
    140–142, 172; communication
    156; flexibility of 122–123;
    individual outpatient treatment
    153–154; intensive outpatient
    treatment 154–155; motivational
    interviewing (MI) 134; non-
    judgmental acknowledgment of
    clients 3; non-vegan therapist
    159; occupational therapist
    8; overgeneralization 163;
    psychodynamic 160; "value
    neutrality" 135; vegan eating
    disordered patients and 142–144;
    vegan therapist 180

therapy: acceptance and
    commitment therapy (ACT)
    132–133, 160; animal therapy
    96–101; group therapy 153;
    individualized treatment
    approach 3; outpatient individual
    therapy 154; *see also* eating
    disorder treatment; non-vegan
    eating disorder treatment;
    therapeutic alliance
Timko, C. A. 53–54
Tunçay, G. Y. 52

University of North Carolina,
    Wilmington 29–30
unspecified feeding or eating
    disorder (UFED) 6

Väänänen, M. 123
vegan informed approach 5, 22,
    111, 146, 166–176; addressing
    secondary trauma and promote
    self-care 175; collaborative
    relationships and participation
    opportunities 172; existing
    frameworks 168; individuals'
    environments context 170;
    prospective 168–175; recovery
    from trauma as a primary goal
    171–172; safe environment,
    creating 169–170; strengths-
    focused perspective 174–175;
    trauma awareness and
    understanding 168–169; trauma-
    informed services 173; trauma
    viewed through a sociocultural
    lens 173–174; universal routine
    screenings for trauma 173
veganism 3–7, 16, 23–24, 28,
    44–45, 103–104, 131; animal
    exploitation and 65, 101; diet
    and 36–38; eating disorders

and 36, 61–63, 108, 146; eating
disorder treatment and 15–20;
ethical 146, 150; losing 86–94;
misconceptions about 2, 32;
professionally considering
113–124; rationale on 42;
restriction and 39, 161–162;
trauma and 70–75, 93, 170;
understanding motivation for,
importance of 47–56; as a value
system 132; in websites 31–32,
34–35; widespread and varied
nature of 32; see also specific
aspects/types
Vegan Society 6, 23, 62, 121, 131,
150, 172

vegetarianism 4, 6–7, 9–10, 44–45;
orthorexia recovery and 50–51;
veganism and 47, 54
Veritas Collaborative 4, 22, 48
Verrastro, Krista 73
vystopia 71, 123
Vystopia: The Anguish of
Being Vegan in a Non-Vegan
World 71, 123

Wendel, B. 7
Wilson, T. D. 103, 106
Wolfram, Taylor 63
Wosket, V. 140, 160

Ziser, K. 134